Maria Gullberg

# CLEVER CROCHET SQUARES

## Artistic Ways to Create Grannies and Dramatic Mosaic Designs

TRAFALGAR SQUARE
North Pomfret, Vermont

First published in the United States of America
in 2019 by
Trafalgar Square Books
North Pomfret, Vermont 05053

Originally published in Swedish as *Virkad mönstermagi*.



ISBN: 978-1-57076-954-2
Library of Congress Control Number: 2019946783

With thanks to:
Hemslöjdens förlag (the original Swedish publisher)
The Swedish National Association of Handicraft Associations
(Svenska Hemslöjdsföreningarnas Riksförbund (SHR))

**Cover** RM Didier
**Projects and Pattern Instructions** Maria Gullberg
**Swedish Publisher's Editor** Cecilia Ljungström
**Photography** Thomas Harrysson
**Drawings** Kalle Forss
**Charts** Cecilia Ljungström
**Fact Checks** Christina Thulin
**Interior Design** Cecilia Ljungström
**Translation into English** Carol Huebscher Rhoades

**Printed in China**
10 9 8 7 6 5 4 3 2 1

# Table of Contents

# Preface

I never would have imagined granny squares would become so precious to me! In my previous book *Tapestry Crochet and More* (Trafalgar, 2016; originally Virka! 2013), I presented a few ideas for how granny squares could be crocheted with new twists; but after that, my train of thought went full speed ahead, and new ideas for constructing the patterns demanded my attention. There was suddenly no limit to the possibilities that popped up, and this book is the result.

My granny squares are based on the classic form, but I thought outside the box as I created my designs. By twisting and turning a square, new alignments and new perspectives present new possibilities. Some of the patterns consist of several blocks that, together, create a repeat. As I worked, I was partly inspired by some of my own tightly-defined graphic design language, and partly by rich folk textile traditions.

If you are holding this book in your hands, you can follow along on a journey that begins at the departure point of classic granny square blocks and then leads further away to new and exciting shapes—a journey that need never end! In this book, you'll find both easy squares and more difficult challenges for those who have already mastered crochet.

I hope you'll find as much creative joy in granny squares as I have!

*Maria Gullberg*

# Crochet Hooks

Crochet hooks can be found in all sorts of materials and designs. I usually work with Boye steel hooks. They lie comfortably in my hand and have a good hook shape. These days, at least in Sweden, it's harder to find Boye hooks in stores; but they still turn up at flea markets and garage sales, and on the internet. Contemporary hooks are typically made of aluminum, plastic, wood, and bamboo. The advantage of metal hooks is they don't bend or break easily. If you don't already have a favorite type of crochet hook, try out a few!

The size (diameter) of the crochet hook can be indicated several ways. There are several systems of hook sizes depending on the kind of materials the hooks are made of and where they are manufactured. In Sweden, for example, the size is given in millimeters (the metric system), while American Boye hooks are sized in an entirely different way. The lower the number a Boye hook has, the larger it is; but the opposite is true in the metric hook size system, where the higher the number, the larger the hook. The size of the crochet hook should be suitable to the yarn it is used with.

## Conversion Chart for Crochet Hooks

| | Number | Number | |
|---|---|---|---|
| Crochet hooks with metric numbering (for example Inoxal, Imra, Aero, Pony brands). | 3-3.5 | 0 | Boye steel hooks.. |
| | 3 | 1 | |
| | 2.5 | 2 | |
| | 2 | 3 | |
| | 1.5 | 4 | |

The size conversions on this table are not exact, but provide general guidance for choosing crochet hooks.

# Stitches

MAGIC RING

Form a ring with the end of the yarn. Insert the crochet hook into the ring, yarn around hook, and pull yarn through ring. Now you have a loop on the hook. Yarn around the hook again and pull it through the loop on the hook. Now you're ready to crochet: work stitches around the ring and then tug on the loose end of the ring to tighten the ring to desired circumference.

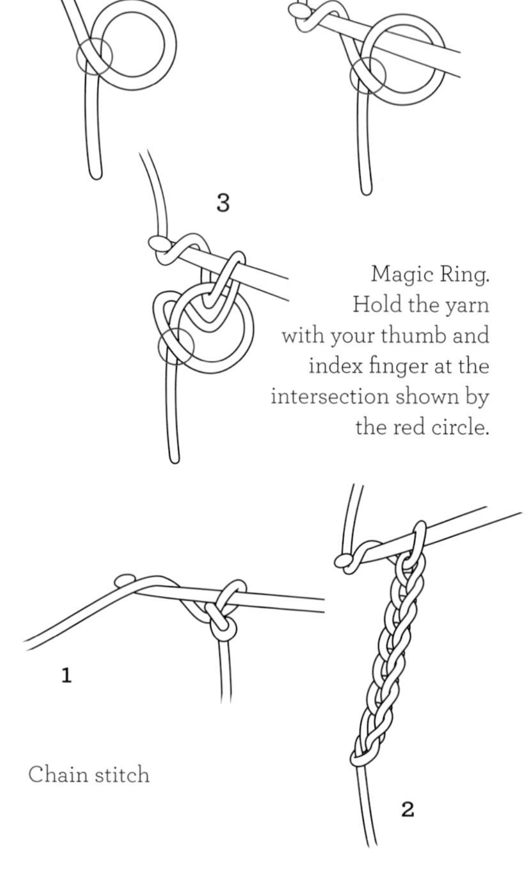


Magic Ring. Hold the yarn with your thumb and index finger at the intersection shown by the red circle.

Chain stitch

CHAIN STITCH (CH ST)

FOUNDATION ROW WITH A LINE OF CHAIN STITCHES

Make a slip knot with the yarn. Insert the hook into the loop, catch the working yarn, and bring it through the loop on the hook. The loop on the hook will be the first in your line of chain stitches. Catch the working yarn and bring it through the loop on the hook. Continue the same way until you have the desired number of chain stitches. Almost all crochet work begins with a foundation chain.

When crocheting into the foundation chain for the first row, there are two ways of inserting the hook into the chain. If you work so the edge of the chain with two strands is on top and the single strand is on the bottom, the foundation will be slightly thicker but not as elastic. If you arrange the strands the opposite way—with the single strand above the hook and two strands below—the foundation will be slightly thinner but more elastic.

YARN OVER HOOK AND YARN AROUND HOOK

A **yarn over hook (yoh)** or a "catch" is the movement you make with the crochet hook to catch the working yarn and bring it through one or more already-worked stitches. A **yarn around hook (yah)** involves wrapping the working yarn once or more around the crochet hook to "build" a particular stitch. For example, see the next page for how to form a double crochet stitch.

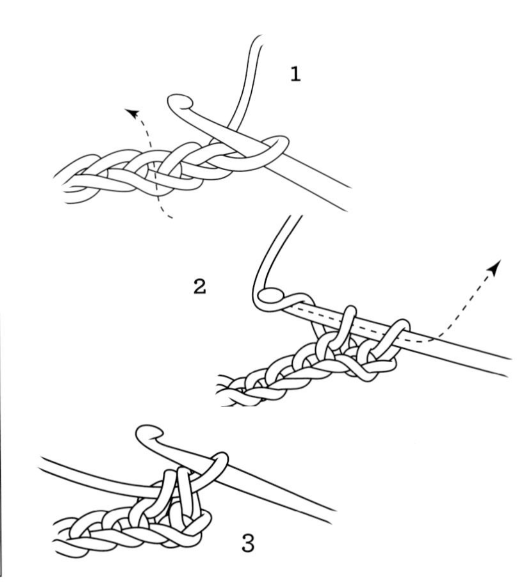


Single crochet

Chain stitches are not only used for foundation chains, but also for patterning with one or more in a row. One or several chain stitches in a row form a chain loop (ch loop).

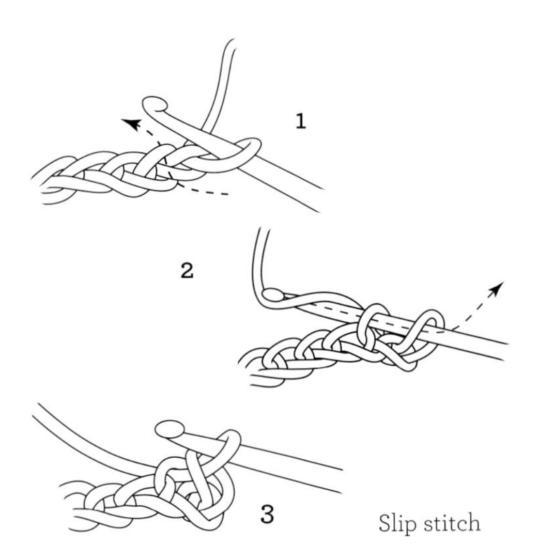


Slip stitch

SLIP STITCH (SL ST)

Insert the hook into a stitch, yarn over hook, and bring it through both the stitch loop and the loop on the hook.

Slip stitches add very little height per row. They are primarily used to join the end of one row/round to the beginning of the previous one, or to move the yarn along a row/round to another place in the crochet sequence.

SINGLE CROCHET (SC)

Insert the hook into a stitch, yarn over hook, and bring strand through the stitch. Now there are two loops on the hook. Yarn over hook again and bring the yarn through both loops on the hook at the same time.

Single (and double) crochet can be worked in several ways: inserting the hook through both loops of the previous row's stitch, through only the front loop of the stitch below, or through only the back loop of the stitch below (or alternating back and front loops). The structure of the crocheted fabric will depend on the method you use.

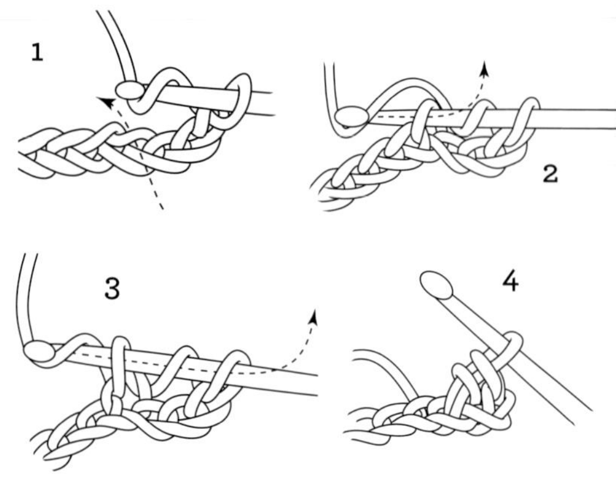

Half double crochet

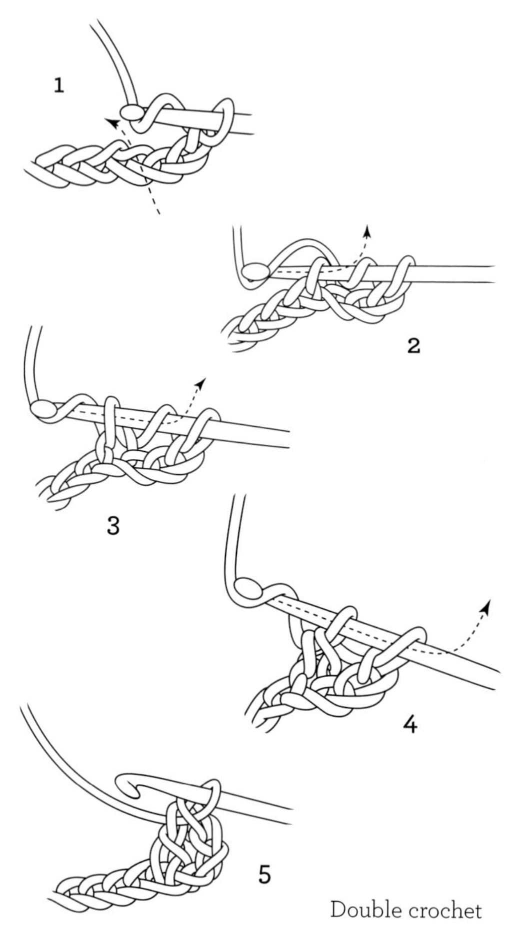

Double crochet

HALF DOUBLE CROCHET (HDC)

Yarn around hook and insert the hook into stitch below, yarn over hook, and bring yarn through stitch loop. Now there are three loops on the hook. Yarn over hook again and bring it through all three loops on the hook at the same time.

DOUBLE CROCHET (DC)

Yarn around hook and then insert the hook into stitch below, yarn over hook, and bring yarn through stitch loop. Now there are three loops on the hook. Yarn over hook again and bring it through the first two of the three loops. Now two loops remain on the hook. Yarn over hook and bring it through the last two loops.

TREBLE CROCHET (TR)

Yarn around hook twice and insert the

hook into stitch below, yarn over hook, and bring yarn through stitch loop. Now there are four loops on the hook. Yarn over hook and bring it through the first two of the four loops. Now three loops remain on the hook. Yarn over hook and bring it through two loops; two loops remain. Yarn over hook and bring it through the last two loops.

Whenever you work a treble or multiple of a treble crochet, the height of the stitch increases for each initial wrap added before working into a stitch. A treble begins with three yarn wraps, a double treble starts with four yarn wraps, and so on. Always bring the yarn through two loops at a time until only one loop remains on the hook.

TURNING CHAIN STITCHES (TCH)

When beginning a new row or round, you need to work one or more chain stitches to reach the right height for the next row. The number of chain stitches required depends on the stitch to be used on the next row. Chain stitches substitute for the first stitch of the next row as follows.

Slip stitches = 1 chain stitch
Single crochet = 2 chain stitches
Half double crochet = 3 chain stitches
Double crochet = 3 chain stitches
Treble crochet = 4 chain stitches

## Symbols

|  |  |
| --- | --- |
| + | Single crochet |
| † | Single crochet for joining blocks |
| (bold †) | Relief stitch |
| T | Half double crochet |
| (T with one slash) | Double crochet |
| (T with two slashes) | Treble crochet |
| (cluster symbol) | 3-double crochet cluster = a cluster (3-dc cl) |
| • | Slip stitch |
| (oval) | Chain stitch |
| (2 stacked ovals) | 2 chain stitches at the beginning of a row/round of single crochet |
| (3 stacked ovals) | 3 chain stitches at the beginning of a row/round of double crochet |

When working in the round, finish each round with a slip stitch in the top chain at the beginning of the round.

# Changing Colors

COLOR CHANGE

To change colors in crochet, use the new color to work the last draw of the yarn through the stitch(es) before the color change.

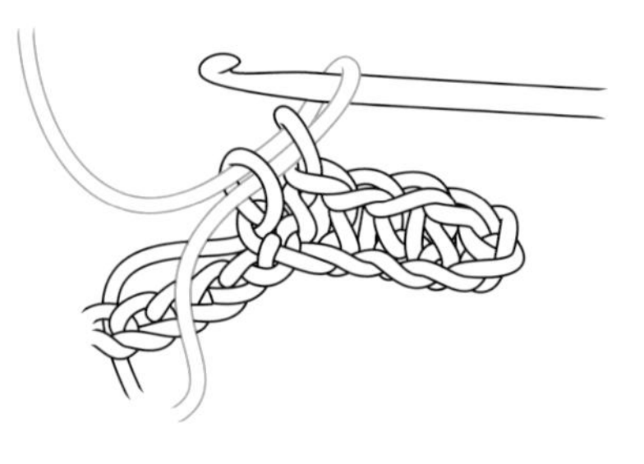

Some blocks of particular patterns (for example, Meetings on page 50) require that you use a different method of changing colors so that the pattern will have distinct edges. This applies to a pattern with two sharply contrasting yarn colors—for example, black and white.

CONTRASTING COLOR CHANGE WITH 3 DOUBLE CROCHETS + 1 CHAIN STITCH

If you want to make a contrast color change when you have a chain stitch between each group of double crochets, work the double crochet group and then change colors at the chain stitch. Work the next double crochet group with the new color and then change colors where the next color change falls in the pattern.

## Crochet Tips

- When you are crocheting with wool yarn and have two colors per row/round, the yarns might tangle as you change colors. If that happens, cut one of the colors, draw the end out of the tangle, and spit-splice the yarn: Fan out each yarn end, overlap the ends, spit (delicately, of course) on the overlapped ends, and then felt the pieces together by rubbing the yarn vigorously between your palms. The moisture and friction will join the strands nicely.

- When crocheting with two colors per row/round, carry the unused color by catching it with the other color as you work. Lay the unused color parallel to and just below the row edge (on the wrong side) to minimize the risk of it becoming visible on the right side. Pull the yarn so it's slightly on the bias and then work into both strands at the same time. Occasionally tug the unused yarn so it won't be too loose, but make sure it doesn't draw in the fabric.

- After a color change, the underlying yarn might show through. To avoid this, on the next row/round, insert the hook under that strand and crochet in/around it as necessary.

- If you are working with various colors but one color isn't needed for a complete row/round, you don't need to carry it around or cut it off. Just leave it at the beginning of the row/round and then pick it up when it's needed again. Make a slip stitch into the first chain stitch of the previous row to catch the waiting yarn and then continue as usual.

- When working with two colors, end/begin the row/round as follows: When working the joining slip stitch in the first stitch of the row with Color A, bring up Color B at the same time and work in/around it. That way, Color B is caught under the stitch and will be at the same height as for Color A when you continue working the next row. Do the same when the ending slip stitch is worked into a chain stitch loop. If you're finished working in a color—or if there are lots of rows/rounds before it's used next—cut the yarn.

# Assembly

Often, squares are joined afterwards by laying them side to side and then joining them with slip stitches or single crochet along the edges. In this book, I chose to join the squares as the work proceeds, so the pattern created across multiple squares won't be disrupted by a joining row added later.

CROCHETING SQUARES TOGETHER AS YOU WORK

Work the first square following the chart. Make the second square up to the last round. To join the two squares, begin at top right in the corner chain loop of the second square and at bottom right in the corner chain loop of the first square. Work 3 double crochet + 1 chain st in the second square, and then a single crochet in the first square. Continue with 3 double crochet in the corner chain loop of the second square, and then a single crochet in the chain loop of the first square.

Make the third square and join it to one of the previous squares as you work the last round.

Make a fourth square and join it to the previous squares as you work the last round. When you come to the point

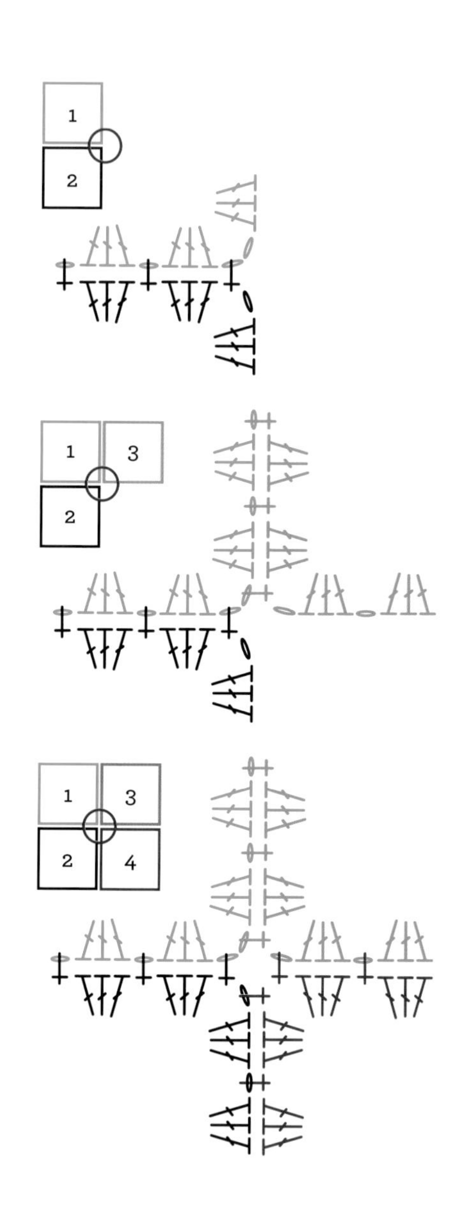


When crocheting squares together, change the chain stitches on the chart for single crochet stitches that are worked in the adjacent square.

where all the squares meet, work the first 3 double crochets in the corner chain loop of the fourth square, and then a single crochet in the corner chain loop of the third square, and a single crochet in the corner chain loop of the second square. Then work 3 double crochets in the corner chain loop of the fourth square.

CROCHETED EDGING AFTER ASSEMBLY

After all the squares have been joined, work a border all around for a fine finish to your work. In each chain loop, work 3 double crochets with 1 chain stitch between each group. Work along the edge in the last square's corner chain loop with 3 double crochets, 1 chain stitch, and 3 double crochets in the next square's first corner chain loop. At the corners, work 3 double crochets + 2 chain stitches + 3 double crochets (see edging on pages 34-35).

An edging can also consist of several rounds of single crochet, or it can be more complex, as for the pillow cover on page 54 (chart on pages 58-59).

FINISHING

Cut the yarn (leaving a short tail) after the last stitch. Draw the end through the stitch using the crochet hook and tighten. Fasten off the end (= weave into the stitches on the wrong side). A good rule of thumb when fastening off is to follow the example shown here with the red strand weaving up and down through the stitch "caps." This method makes the ends nearly invisible. You can also "fasten off" by threading the yarn end into a blunt-tip tapestry needle and working up and down through the stitches.

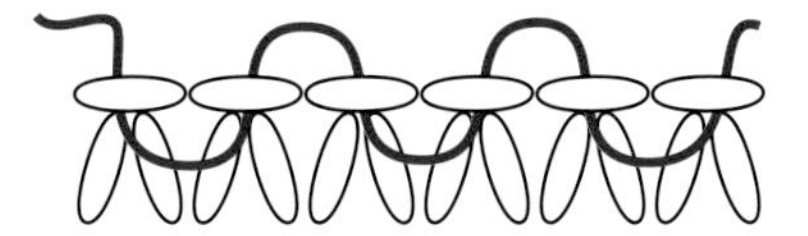

Here's how to fasten off a yarn end. The illustration shows a row of single crochet.

BLOCKING AND PRESSING THE FINISHED PIECE

Pin out the piece and lightly dampen it with water from a spray bottle and then leave it until completely dry. If there's no texture in the pattern, you could also block the piece by gently steam pressing it under a damp pressing cloth. If you've made a large coverlet, it might be hard to pin it out unless you have a large blocking surface—it's easier to block sections of the blanket as you work on it.

# Projects

With all the many fantastic patterns in this book, you can make all kinds of fine work. A little further in the book, for example, I'll discuss how the Miss Flower design can become a **pillow cover**. Adastra or Stripe can be shaped into a **bag**, and Armida into a **mat**. And, of course, you can make pillow covers, bags, and mats with whatever pattern motif you like. You can even make **coverlets** and **baby blankets**. Or perhaps a **chair cover**? Here's a good tip for making a chair cover: once you've crocheted the cover, make an edging of small squares consisting of 2-3 rounds. Crochet these edging squares to the top section and use leather, *vadmal* (fabric that's woven and then felted), or felt for the underside of the cover. If you use strong cotton yarn, the squares in the Circular pattern would make nice **potholders**.

SIZING THE SQUARES

In the introduction to the instructions, you'll find information about how to size individual squares. I crochet pretty firmly, and that's what the measurements of the squares are based on; the numbers will be different if you work more loosely. Be smart before you begin a project and make a swatch so you'll know what the end result will be. If you crochet too loosely, you can adjust by tensioning the working yarn more tightly (for example, don't just lay it over your index finger but weave it under your middle finger and over your ring finger), or change to a smaller hook. If you crochet too tightly, try changing to a larger hook.

YARN AMOUNTS

If you want to crochet a larger projects, it's a good idea to calculate how much yarn you'll need. Choose the yarn you want and weigh it. Crochet a square or as many squares as needed for a repeat. Now weigh the remaining yarn and write down how many grams you used. Figure out how many squares or repeats you are going to make for the entire project and multiply that total by the grams per piece. When you know how many grams of each color you'll need, you can calculate how many skeins you'll have to buy. Don't forget to add extra for edgings, assembly, and finishing. Always keep in mind that it's a good idea to have a little more than you need, just in case!

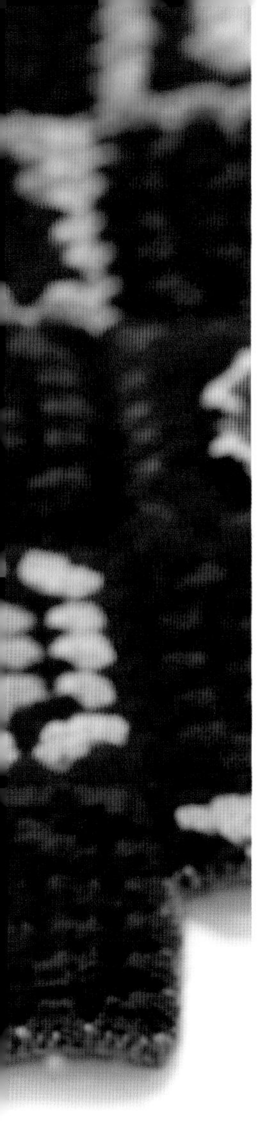

# Granny Squares

Easy

**Finished Measurements**
One square measures 3¼ x 3¼ in / 8 x 8 cm.

MATERIALS
**Yarn:**
CYCA #2 (sport/baby) 6/2 wool yarn (100% wool, 330 yd/302 m / 100 g)

**Yarn Colors:**
My color selection: assorted leftover yarn colors.
**Crochet Hook:** U. S. size B-1 or C-2 / 2.5 mm: Aero or similar style hook.

It's easy to get underway with your crocheting with a classic granny square.

Begin each square with a magic ring or ch 6 and close into a ring with 1 sl st.

Now make the squares following the charts on pages 18-19 and 22- 23. Make some subdued squares with a few well-chosen shades, or do as I have and play with all sorts of colors. You can even vary the squares by working with relief stitches and single crochet (see Charts 3 and 4 on page 19), or by later attaching "special effects," such as small flower squares. The squares are joined with each other on the last round of each.

On the following pages, you'll find crochet charts with suggestions for various color combinations and stitches. If you want all your squares to be the same size, keep in mind that a round of double crochet corresponds to two rounds of single crochet. All the single-crochet rounds are worked into the previous round's back loops.

Granny Square, Chart 1

Granny Square, Chart 2

The chart shows a classic granny square. If you want, you can make a colorful square and change colors on every round. If changing colors on every round, you can skip across all the slip stitches besides those joining the round.

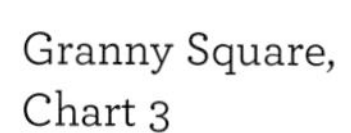

Granny Square, Chart 3

All the single and double crochet stitches are worked over the double crochets in the previous round with the single crochet stitches worked through the back loops.

Granny Square, Chart 4

All the single crochet stitches are worked over double crochets of the previous round through the back loops.

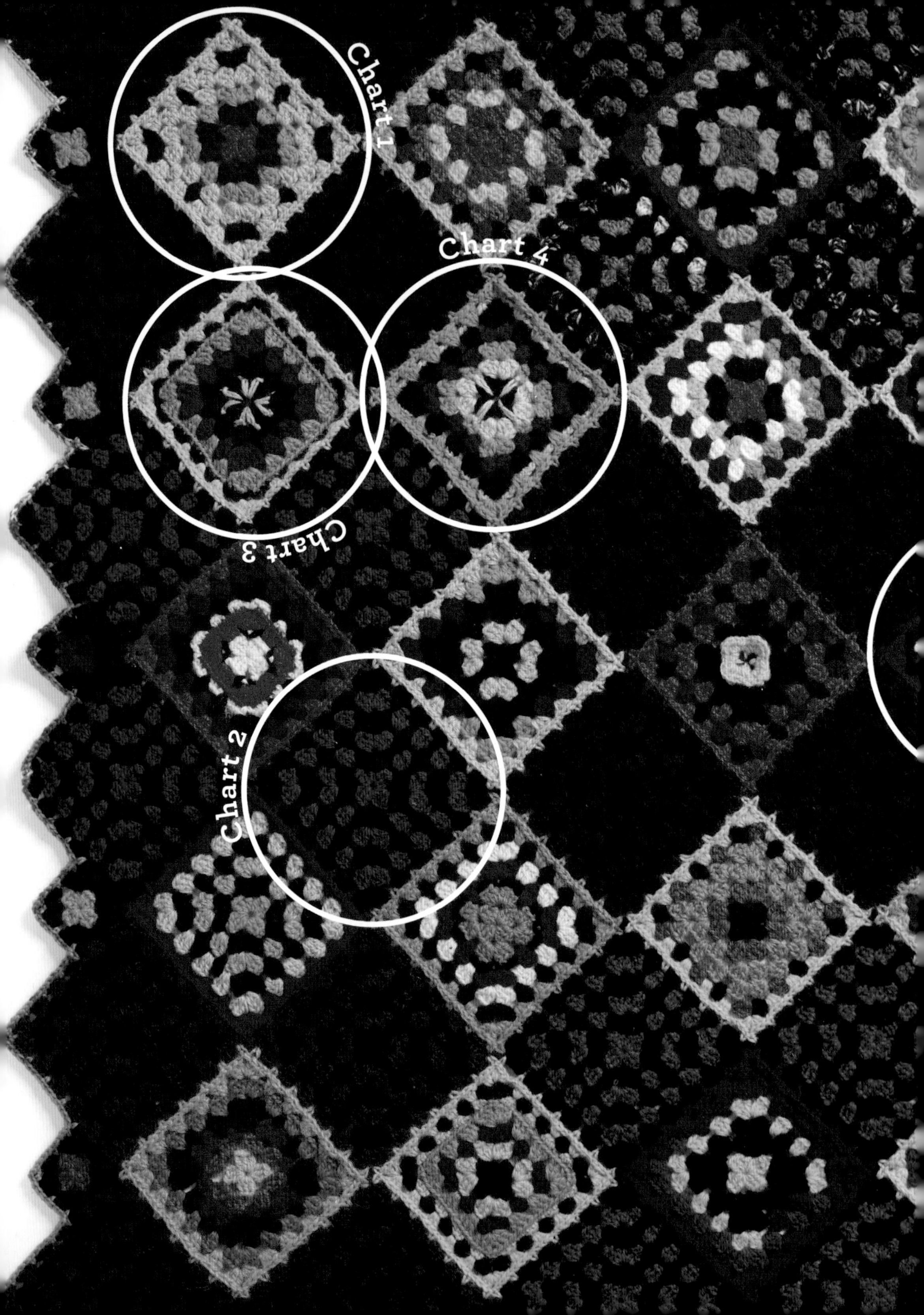
Chart 1
Chart 4
Chart 3
Chart 2

Chart 5
Chart 6
Chart 7

Granny Square, Chart 5

On Rnd 4, the corner chain loops shift by a quarter turn.

## Flower Center

"The Flower" is crocheted onto the fabric's right side afterwards. Insert the hook into the center of a square and through one corner chain loop on the first round. Work 1 sc + ch 3. Repeat this in every chain corner around the center circle. Finish with 1 sl st into the first st. On the next round, work (1 sc, 1 hdc, 2 dc, 1 hdc, 1 sc) in each chain loop. Finish with 1 sl st into the first st. Cut yarn.

Granny Square, Chart 6

All the single and double crochets are worked over the double crochets of the previous round with the single crochet stitches worked through back loops.

On the rounds where you work 3 chain stitches followed by 1 single crochet, the single crochet stitches are worked into the chain loop of the previous round.

Granny Square, Chart 7

### Project: Coverlet

Making coverlets with granny squares is nothing new, but by assembling the squares in specific patterns, you can create something truly eye-catching. I worked the darker squares following Chart 2 and used them as a background to emphasize the more colorful squares. By assembling the squares on the diagonal (see schematic), I gave the coverlet pointed edges. I made the edging extra fine by adding small two-round squares into the notches. Finally, I crocheted a round of single crochet all around the coverlet and decorated the corners with tassels. When working a finished round with single crochet stitches, work 1 single crochet in one square's corner chain loop and 1 single crochet in the second square's corner chain loop at each inward-facing corner. At an outward-facing corner, work (1 sc, ch 2, 1 sc) into the corner chain loop.

1. Join two dark squares on the diagonal.

2. Join four dark squares together on the diagonal.

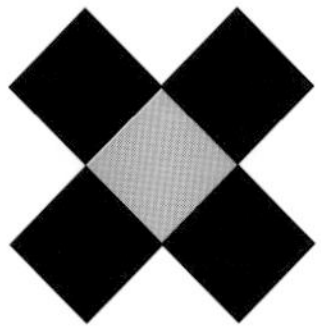

3. Crochet a multi-color square in the center.

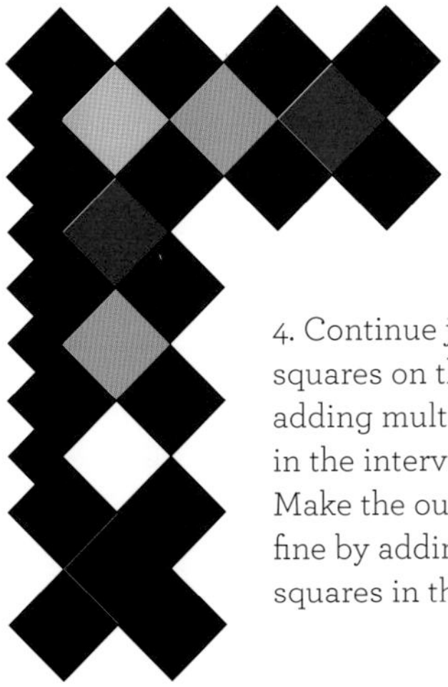

4. Continue joining dark squares on the diagonal, adding multi-color squares in the intervening spaces. Make the outer edge extra fine by adding small squares in the notches.

### Yarn Tassels

Cut about 2.7 yd / 2.5 m yarn (how much depends on how thick your yarn is) and double the strand. Catch the ends in the corner chain loop of an edge square; wrap the yarn around three fingers held together, and then into the chain loop again. Repeat the process until the yarn is used up. Remove your fingers and wind a bit of yarn a few wraps around the top of the tassel. Fasten by sewing back and forth through the wraps a couple of times. Cut the yarn ends, hide them in the tassel, and trim tassel.

# Botilda

Easy

**Finished Measurements**
One square measures 3½ x 3½ in / 9 x 9 cm.

**MATERIALS**
**Yarn:**
CYCA #2 (sport/baby) 6/2 wool yarn (100% wool, 330 yd/302 m / 100 g)

**Yarn Colors:**
My color selection: black, red, white, and assorted shades of blue.
**Crochet Hook:** U. S. size B-1 or C-2 / 2.5 mm: Aero or similar style hook.

The idea for this piece was taken from a weaving.

Begin each square with a magic ring or ch 6 and close into a ring with 1 sl st.

Now make the squares following Chart 1 on the next page, working with your choice of colors.

While working Rnd 6, join the squares following the basic instructions on page 12. If you want to reproduce the pattern in the photo, join the squares four by four and then crochet an edging around each group (see chart on the next page). Crochet these larger squares together, and end with a round of single crochet all around the entire piece. Weave in all ends neatly on wrong side.

**Edging Panel:** Crochet an edging around four joined squares following the chart on the next page. In the notch between two squares, work 3 dc in the last corner chain loop of the first square, and then ch 1 followed by 3 dc in the first corner chain loop of the second square.

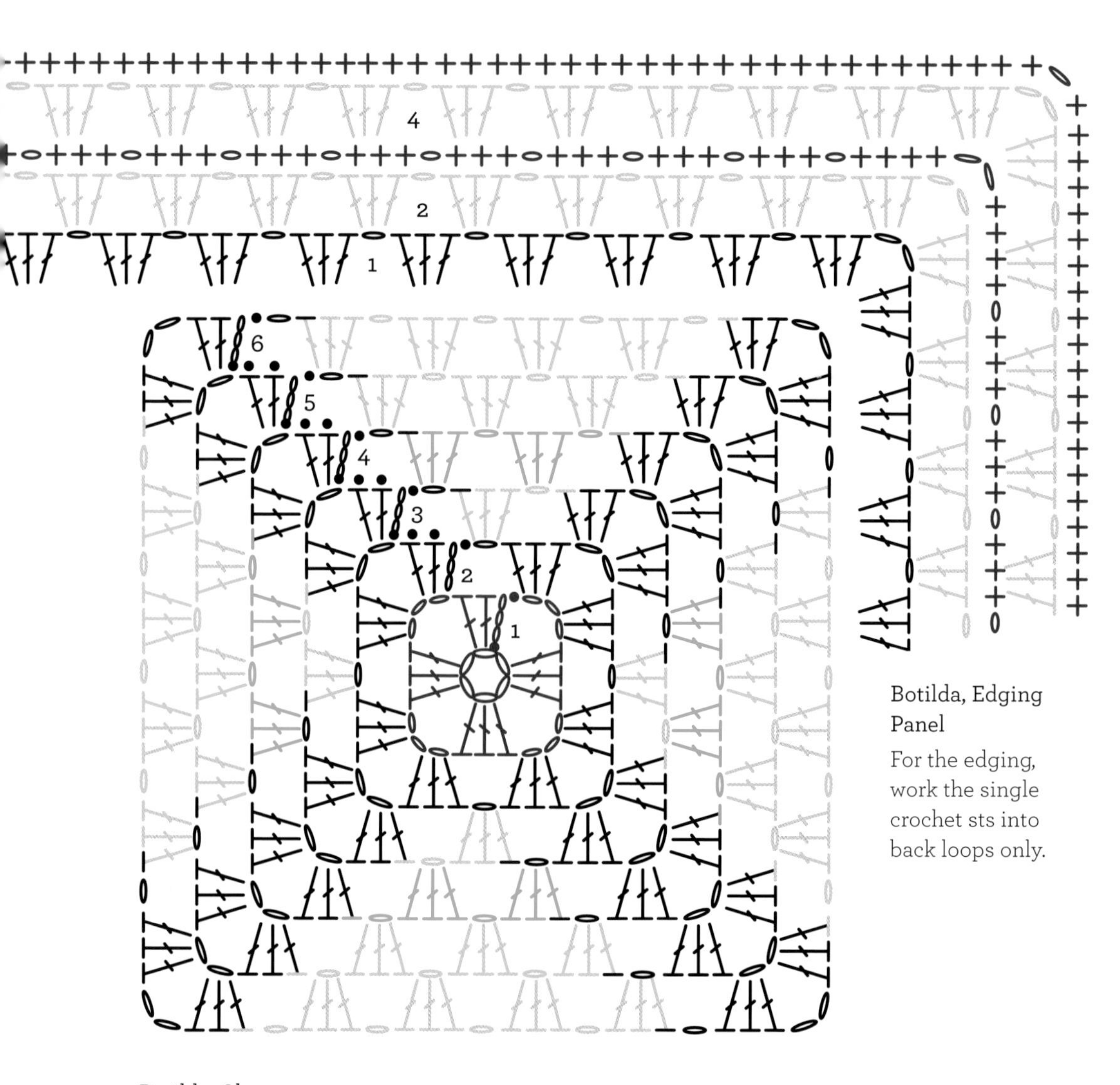


Botilda, Edging Panel

For the edging, work the single crochet sts into back loops only.

Botilda, Chart 1

One repeat consists of four joined crochet squares that are then edged. To make the second color sequence as shown in the photo on page 26, flip the colors: black and white change places, as do blue and red.

Botilda, Chart 2

A suggestion for an alternate color arrangement. You can see the crocheted pattern without the edging panel on pages 30-31.

# Ruth Block

Easy

**Finished Measurements**
One square measures 3½ x 3½ in / 9 x 9 cm.

**MATERIALS**
**Yarn:**
CYCA #2 (sport/baby) 6/2 wool yarn (100% wool, 330 yd/302 m / 100 g)

**Yarn Colors:**
My color selection: light gray, black and an assortment of leftover colors.
**Crochet Hook:** U. S. size B-1 or C-2 / 2.5 mm: Aero or similar style hook.

I took the idea for this piece from a folk weaving.

Begin each square with a magic ring or ch 6 and close into a ring with 1 sl st.

Now make the squares following the chart on page 35.

Choose between two ways of using the black yarn.

**Alternative 1:** On Rnds 3 and 5, let the black yarn "rest" at the beginning of the round—do not carry it around. On Rnds 4 and 6, carry the black yarn and catch it with the gray yarn until it's time to use it.

**Alternative 2:** For the black sections (Rnds 4 and 6), cut 4 black strands, each about 60 in / 150 cm long. Crochet from the center of a black strand on Rnd 4 and use the beginning of the strand for Rnd 6. Consider carrying the gray yarn around to catch under the black stitches.

When working Rnd 6, join squares following the basic instructions on page 12. Finish by weaving in all ends neatly on wrong side.

**Edging Panel:** If you want to make a pillow cover or perhaps a throw with your joined Ruth squares, a crocheted edging all around the piece is a nice finishing touch. This edging consists of only one round crocheted with black yarn. In the notches between the squares, work 3 dc in the last corner chain loop of the first square, and then ch 1 + 3 dc in the first corner chain loop of the next square.

### Pompoms

Wrap the yarn about 10 times over three fingers held together (index/middle/ring) and then, with linen lace yarn or strong sewing thread, tie a very firm knot around the center of the bundle. Sew a pompom in the center of the gray section. Cut the yarn and trim the ends to about 3/8 in / 1 cm.

Edging for the Ruth Blocks

Ruth Block Chart

# Twill

Intermediate to Experienced

**Finished Measurements**
One square measures 3½ x 3½ in / 9 x 9 cm.

**MATERIALS**
**Yarn:**
CYCA #2 (sport/baby) 6/2 wool yarn (100% wool, 330 yd/302 m / 100 g)

**Yarn Colors:**
My color selection: Black, various shades of gray and red for special effect.
**Crochet Hook:** U. S. size B-1 or C-2 / 2.5 mm: Aero or similar style hook.

The idea for this design was inspired by a twill weaving that caught my eye when I was looking for a graphic look with contrasting light and dark shades as the theme. The repeat for the pattern is mirror-image on every other lengthwise repeat, in order to create a recurring rhythm in the pattern.

Begin each square with a magic ring or ch 6 and close into a ring with 1 sl st.

Now make the squares following the charts on the next two pages. Each square consists of a total of 6 rounds and is worked with 2 colors per round throughout.

Begin by working the desired number of squares following Chart 1. Join the squares vertically as you work Rnd 6, following the basic instructions on page 12. Next, make the same number of squares following Chart 2, and join them vertically as you work Rnd 6.

Make as many vertical rows of squares as you want, and then sew them together using a contrast color. Sew with right sides held together, using 4-5 whip stitches in each chain loop.

Finish by weaving in all ends neatly on wrong side.

Twill, Chart 1

Chart 1 and Chart 2 are joined with whip stitch through the stitch loops.
Chart 1 is tilted by a half-turn.

Twill, Chart 2

# The ’50s

Easy to Intermediate

**Finished Measurements**
One square measures 3½ x 3½ in / 9 x 9 cm.

MATERIALS

**Yarn:**
CYCA #2 (sport/baby) 6/2 wool yarn (100% wool, 330 yd/302 m / 100 g)

**Yarn Colors:**
My color selection: black, red, and pale green.

**Crochet Hook:** U. S. size B-1 or C-2 / 2.5 mm: Aero or similar style hook.

The colors and designs of the 1950s inspired this pattern.

Begin each square with a magic ring or ch 6 and close into a ring with 1 sl st.

Now make the squares following the chart on the next page. Make several squares, some with red at the center and others centered with the main color.

Join the squares as you work Rnd 6 following the basic instructions on page 12. Finish by weaving in all ends neatly on wrong side.

The 1950s Chart

The ’50s, assembled

In order to create this pattern, work every other square with pale green in the center instead of red.

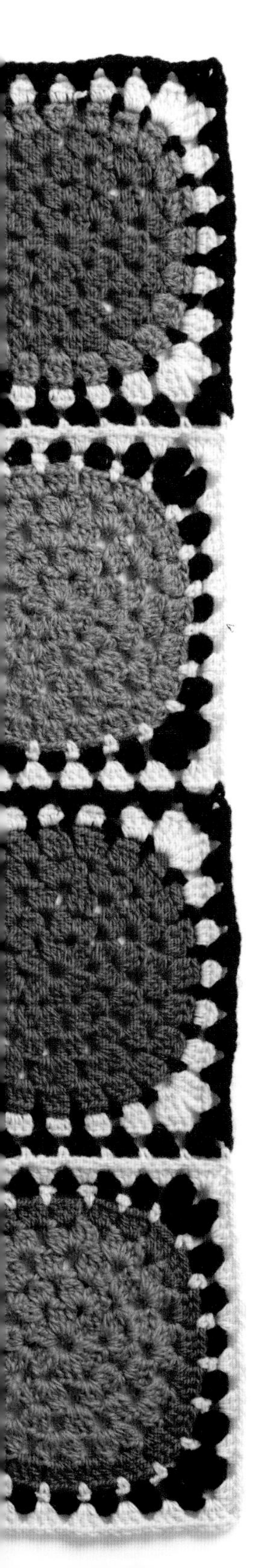

# Raffle

Easy

**Finished Measurements**
One square measures 4¾ x 4¾ in / 12 x 12 cm.

**MATERIALS**

**Yarn:**
CYCA #2 (sport/baby) 6/2 wool yarn (100% wool, 330 yd/302 m / 100 g)

**Yarn Colors:**
My color selection: black, white, blue-turquoise, and orange.

**Crochet Hook:** U. S. size B-1 or C-2 / 2.5 mm: Aero or similar style hook.

The idea for this design was derived from an African printed fabric, but the color choices give the piece a 1950s look.

Begin each square with a magic ring or ch 6 and close into a ring with 1 sl st.

Now make the squares following the chart on page 48. Play with a variety of color options to bring out different aspects of the pattern.

Make several squares and crochet them together while working Rnd 8 following the basic instructions on page 12. Finish by weaving in all ends neatly on wrong side.

# Special

Intermediate to Experienced

**Finished Measurements**
One square measures 4¾ x 4¾ in / 12 x 12 cm.

**MATERIALS**

**Yarn:**
CYCA #2 (sport/baby) 6/2 wool yarn (100% wool, 330 yd/302 m / 100 g)

**Yarn Colors:**
My color selection: black, white, blue tonal, silver effect yarn.

**Crochet Hook:** U. S. size B-1 or C-2 / 2.5 mm: Aero or similar style hook.

This square is an offshoot of the Raffle square (see page 45). The difference is that this square has a patterned edging crocheted with two colors per round.

Begin each motif with a magic ring or ch 6 and close into a ring with 1 sl st.

Now make the squares following the chart on page 49. On the chart, the red color corresponds to the silver thread you can see worked into the finished project shown here.

Make several squares and crochet them together while working Rnd 9 following the basic instructions on page 12. Finish by weaving in all ends neatly on wrong side.

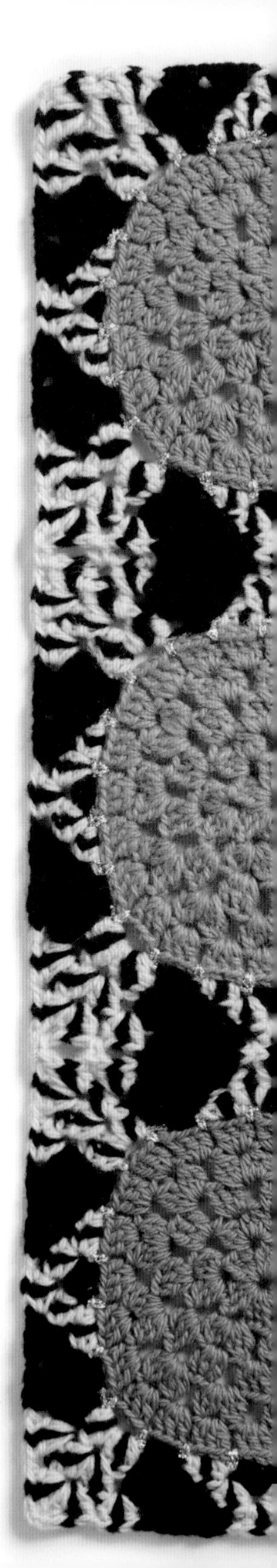

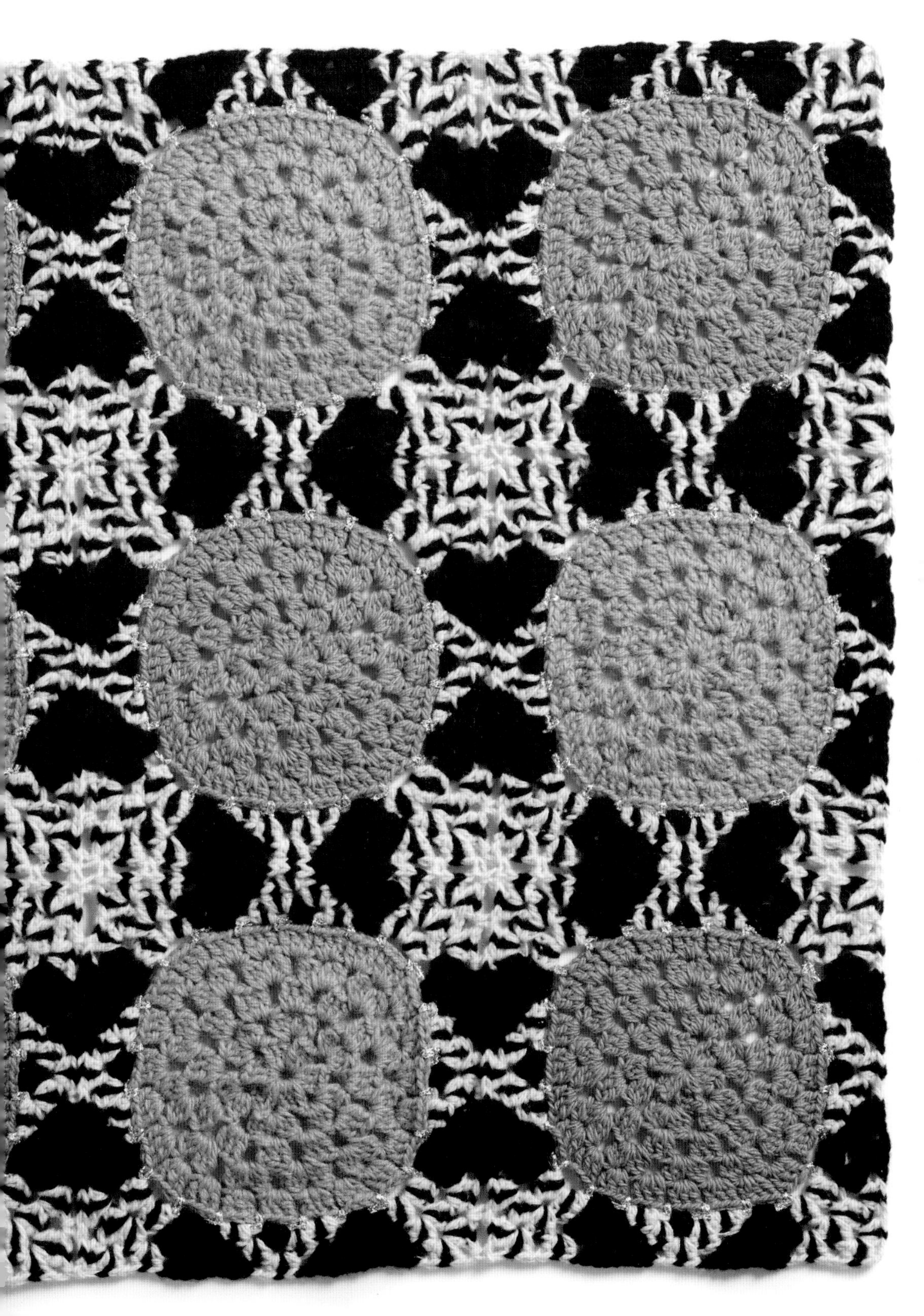

Raffle Chart

When I crocheted the Raffle motif, I varied the color of the central circle and sometimes used colors from another square for the last round. For the square's final three rounds, I arranged the colors as either black-white-black or white-black-white.

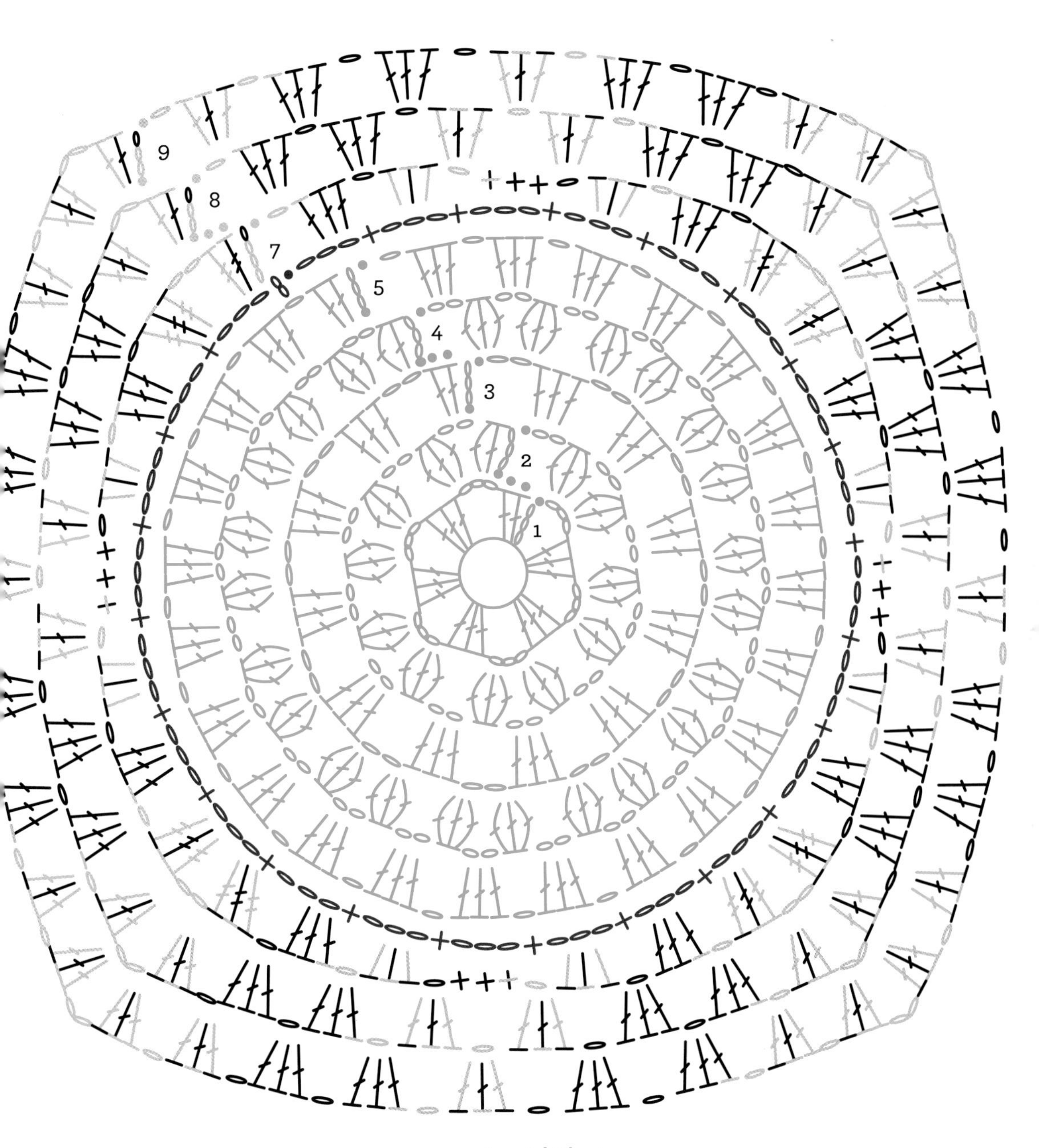


Special Chart

On Rnds 7, 8, and 9 of Special, work the color changes firmly. The red round on the sketch above corresponds to the silver effect thread you can see in the photo on page 47.

# Meetings

Intermediate to Experienced

**Finished Measurements**
One square measures 4¾ x 4¾ in / 12 x 12 cm.

**MATERIALS**
**Yarn:**
CYCA #2 (sport/baby) 6/2 wool yarn (100% wool, 330 yd/302 m / 100 g)

**Yarn Colors:**
My color selection: black, white, and assorted colors.
**Crochet Hook:** U. S. size B-1 or C-2 / 2.5 mm: Aero or similar style hook.

Kaleidoscope patterns inspired this design.

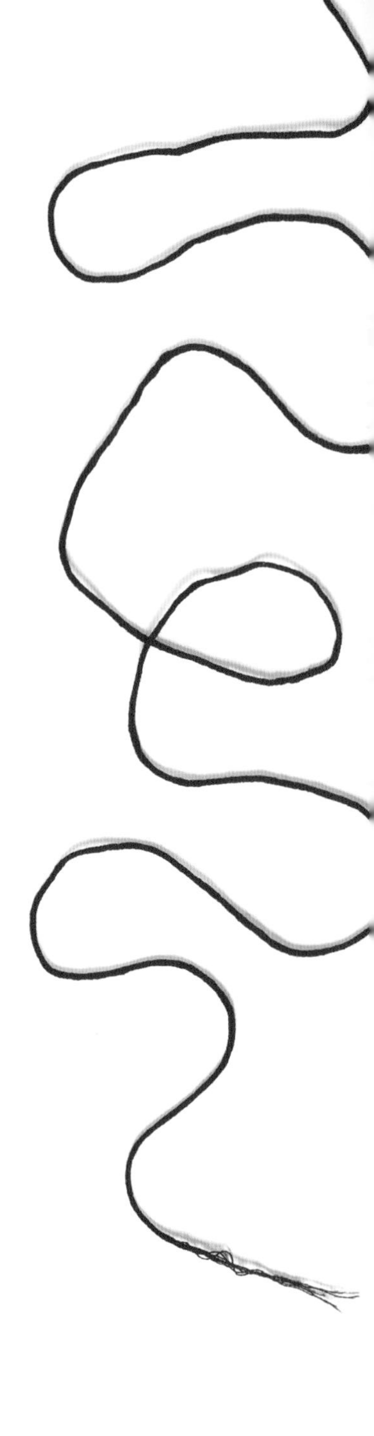

Begin each motif with a magic ring or ch 6 and close into a ring with 1 sl st.

Now make the squares following the chart opposite. To make the pattern more even, work the color changes the "alternate" way on Rnd 8 (see page 10). Make several squares, varying the color on whichever color round you want or using the same color in all the squares. Crochet the squares together while working Rnd 8 following the basic instructions on page 12. Turn the squares (see illustration) to create a pattern. Finish by weaving in all ends neatly on wrong side.

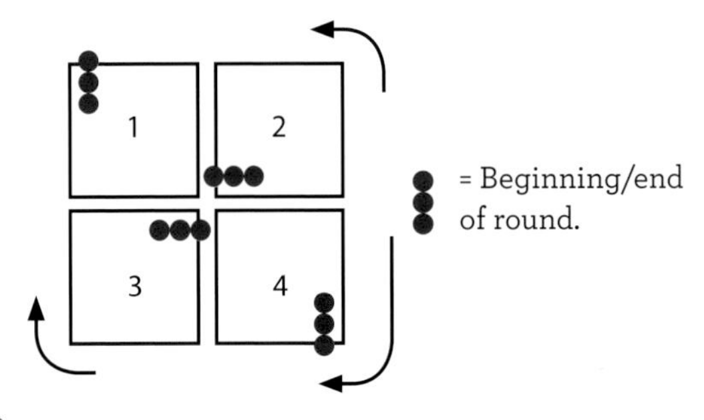

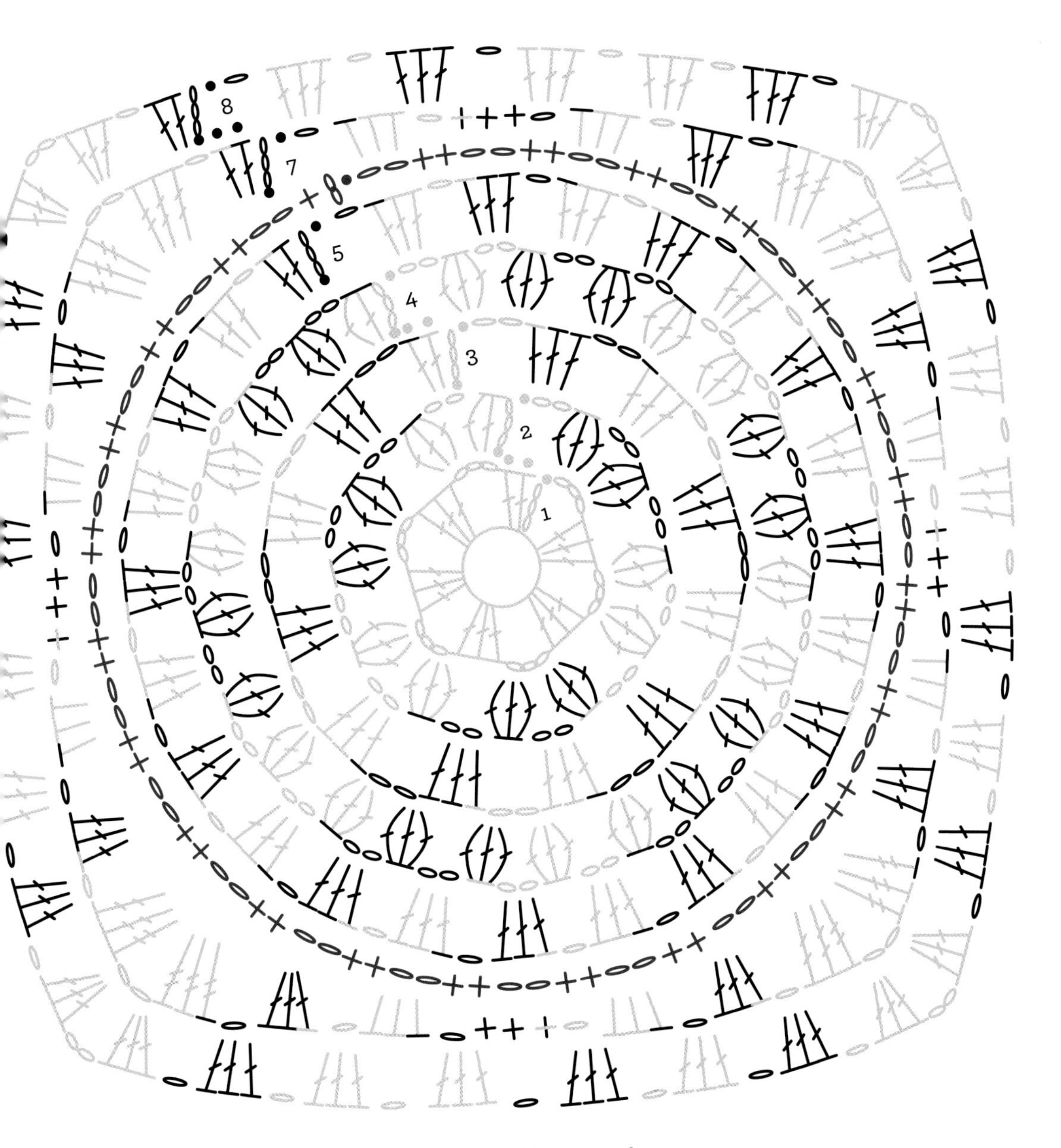


Meetings Chart

When you crochet the squares together on Rnd 8, work the color changes in the final step of the single crochet stitches worked in the adjoining square's chain loop.

# Miss Flower

Intermediate

**Finished Measurements**
One square measures 3½ x 3½ in / 9 x 9 cm..

**MATERIALS**
**Yarn:**
CYCA #2 (sport/baby) 6/2 wool yarn (100% wool, 330 yd/302 m / 100 g)
**Yarn Colors:**
My color selection: black and turquoise as the background colors with a variety of colors for the flowers.

**Crochet Hook:** U. S. size B-1 or C-2 / 2.5 mm: Aero or similar style hook.
**Notions:** Pillow form slightly larger than pillow cover; pieces of black lining fabric and *vadmal* or felt the same dimensions as pillow cover; matching sewing thread. Optional: gold and silver sequins.

Folk embroidery and garden plants combined to provide the inspiration for this design.

Begin each square with a magic ring or ch 6 and close into a ring with 1 sl st.

Now make the squares following the chart on page 57. Make several squares, preferably with the "flowers" in a variety of colors.

Crochet the squares together while working Rnd 8 following the basic instructions on page 12. Finish by weaving in all ends neatly on wrong side.

**Project: Pillow Cover**
Make 16 squares and assemble them into a square block. Crochet an edging all around (see chart on pages 58-59). If desired, sew a gold **sequin** to the center of each flower and silver sequins in the centers of Rnds 6-8 of the edging.

Cut a backing for the cover out of ***vadmal*** (woven fabric that has been felted) or felt and a lining of **black cotton fabric** the same measurements as the pillow cover. With right side facing right side, machine-stitch the felted piece to the cotton lining fabric with a 3/8 in / 1 cm seam allowance. Leave an opening about 8 in / 20 cm on one of the sides. Press the seam allowance open and turn the cover right side out. Place the crocheted front over the black cotton fabric, with the last two rounds of crocheted edging sticking out as pointed tips around the pillow. Pin or baste the crocheted front and then use sewing thread to sew it securely with invisible stitching in the last double crochet row, inserting the needle down into the seam or just outside the felted piece. Make sure the crocheted front lies smooth and flat.

Insert the **pillow form**, which should be slightly larger than the cover so it will fill out the corners well. Finally, seam the remaining opening with invisible stitching.

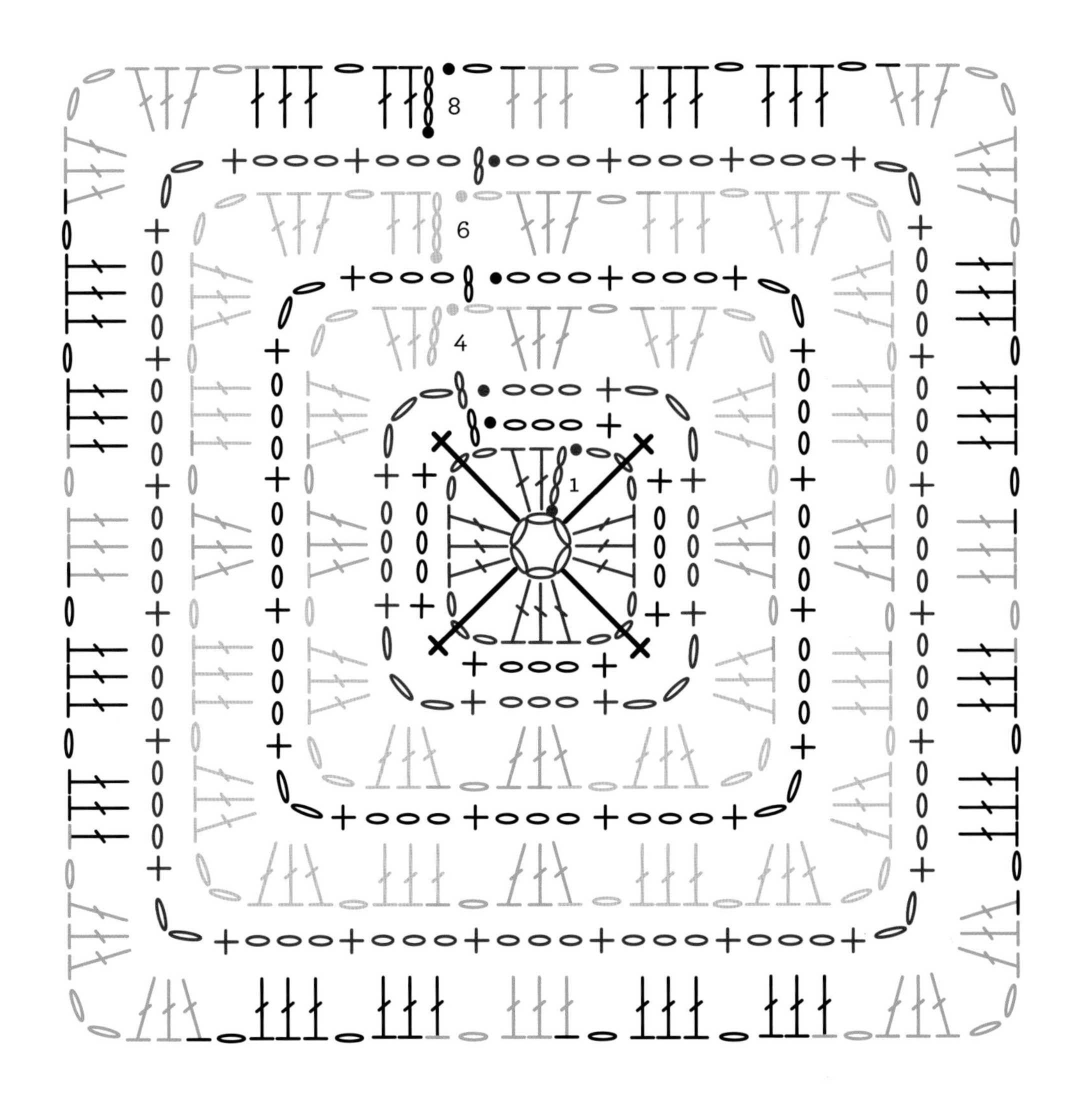


Miss Flower Chart

When crocheting Miss Flower, you can vary the colors on the yellow and red stitches on the chart so you'll have "flowers" of different colors.

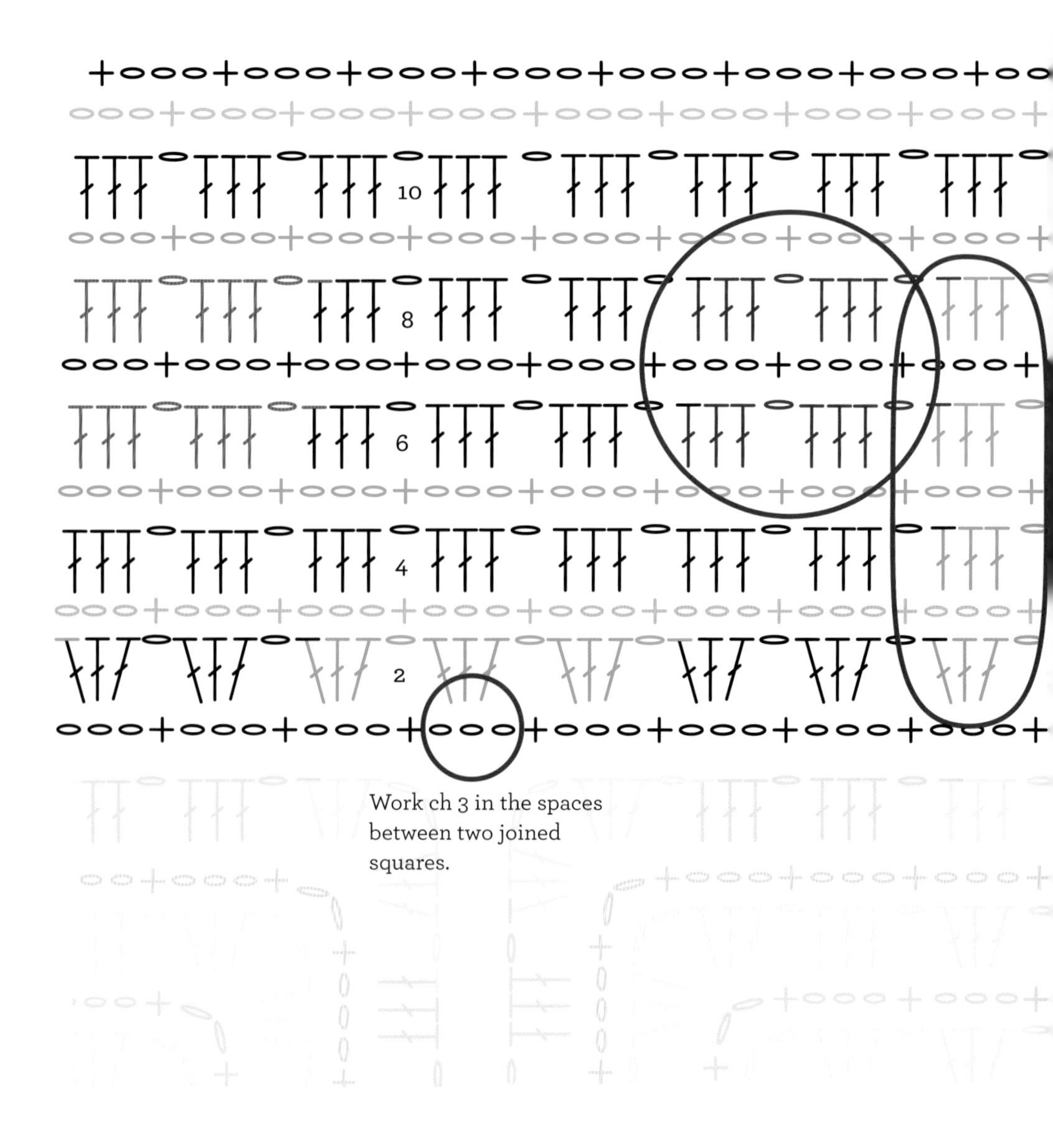


Work ch 3 in the spaces between two joined squares.

On the sections with two different colors over two rounds, you can cut a strand about 60 in / 150 cm long (for the color section in the corner, you'll need about 83 in / 210 cm). Crochet from the center of the strand on Rnd 1 and use the beginning of the strand for Rnd 2.

For the sections with blue over four rounds, you can cut a strand about 60 in / 150 cm long. Begin crocheting with one end of the strand.

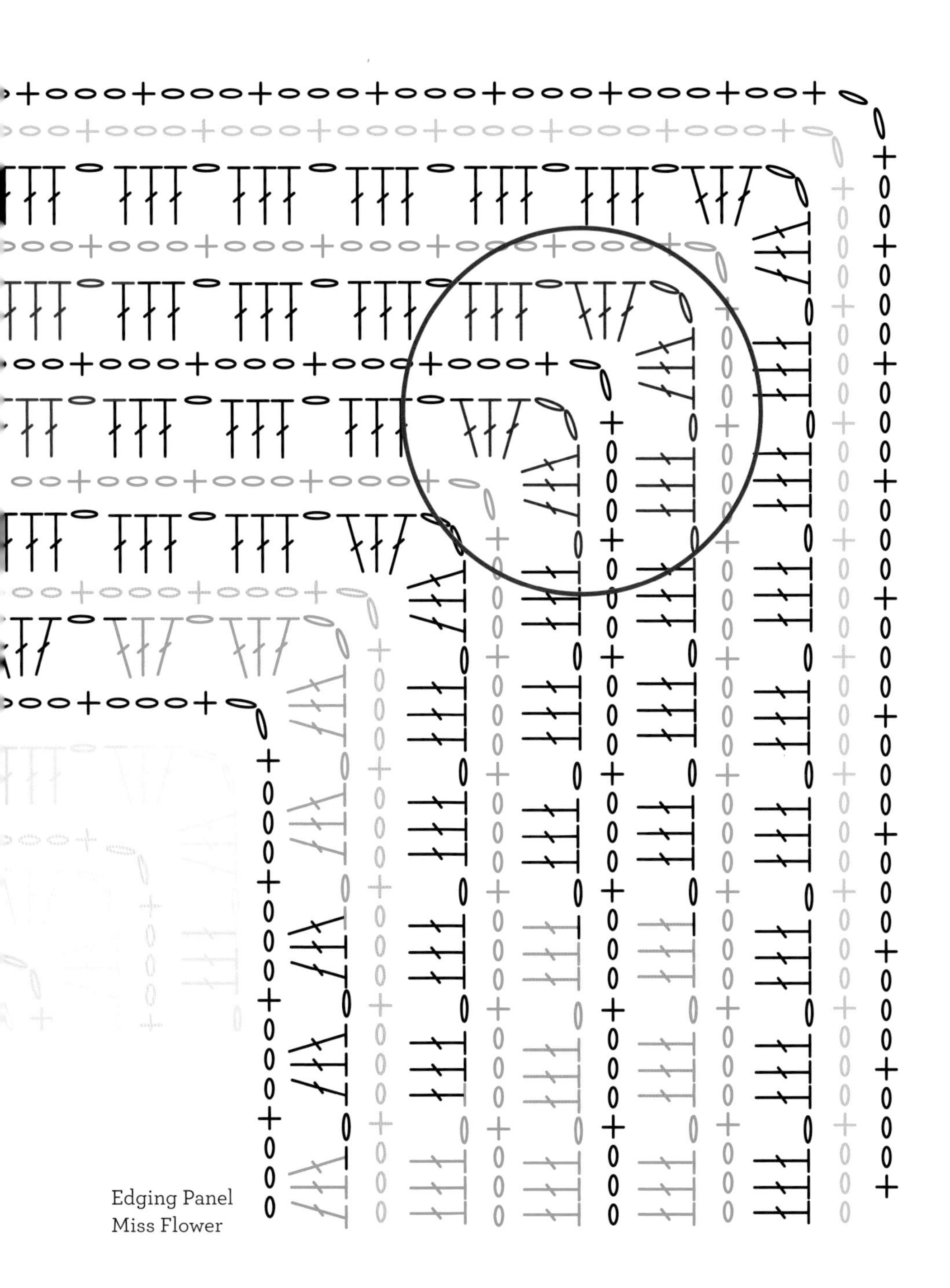

Edging Panel
Miss Flower

# A Small Cog

Intermediate

**Finished Measurements**
One square measures 2½ x 2½ in / 6 x 6 cm.

MATERIALS
**Yarn:**
CYCA #2 (sport/baby) 6/2 wool yarn (100% wool, 330 yd/302 m / 100 g)

**Yarn Colors:**
My color selection: mole-skin, red, black, and white.
**Crochet Hook:** U. S. size B-1 or C-2 / 2.5 mm: Aero or similar style hook.

My idea for this design originated in Swedish folk pattern traditions.

Begin each square with a magic ring or ch 6 and close into a ring with 1 sl st.

Now make the first square following Chart 1 on the next page. Continue with Chart 2 and then Chart 3. For a complete pattern repeat, you'll need to crochet one square following Chart 1, four from Chart 2, and four from Chart 3.

Alternate the colors of the squares or make them all the same sequence—as you like.

Crochet the squares together while working Rnd 4 following the basic instructions on page 12. Finish by weaving in all ends neatly on wrong side.

A Small Cog, Chart 1

A Small Cog, Chart 2

On Rnds 2, 3, and 4, use the alternate color change method rather than the traditional method (see page 10).

A Small Cog, Chart 3

A Small Cog, one pattern repeat

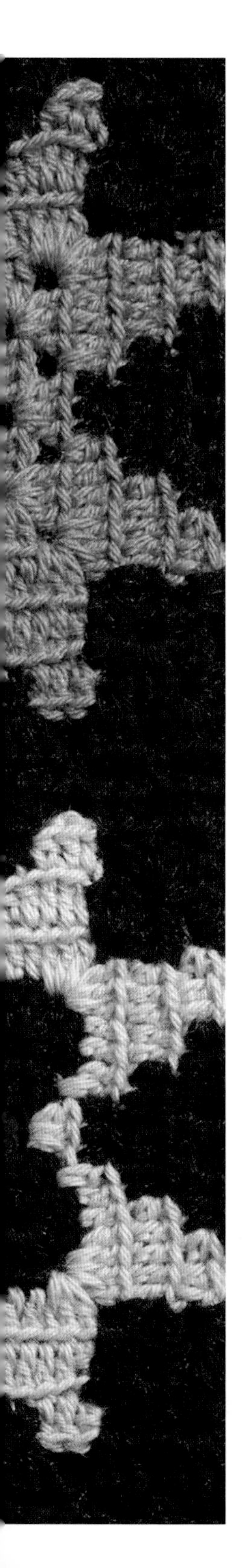

# Adastra

Intermediate

**Finished Measurements**
One square measures 3½ x 3½ in / 9 x 9 cm.

MATERIALS
**Yarn:**
CYCA #1 (fingering) 18/4 wool yarn (100% wool, 492 yd/450 m / 100 g)
**Yarn Colors:**
My color selection: red, blue, ochre, green, black, and natural white.
**Crochet Hook:** U. S. size D-3 / 3 mm: Aero or similar style hook.
**Notions:** Pieces of leather to match dimensions of bag (see details in instructions below). To match dimensions of bag + 3/8 in / 1 cm seam allowance all around each of: cotton fabric, two pieces of red and one piece of black; and one piece iron-on vlieseline interfacing. Matching sewing thread. Cotton yarn. Canvas band, approx. 1½ in / 4 cm wide and 51¼ in / 130 cm long for shoulder strap facing. Matching sewing thread. Revolving punch pliers.
**Optional:** Cardboard piece to reinforce base of bag and lining fabric to cover cardboard; hand-twisted or purchased cord to embellish bag.

Wool embroidery from Skåne (the south of Sweden) inspired this design.

Begin each square with a magic ring or ch 6 and close into a ring with 1 sl st.

Now make a square following Chart 1 on page 66. All of the double crochet stitches are worked into the back loops of the previous round's double crochets. Create different "stars" by making a variety of center pieces (see charts 2 and 3 on page 67). Play with a variety of colors also.

The squares are crocheted together vertically as you work. Join squares as you work Rnd 7 following the basic instructions on page 12. Crochet the vertical strips together using an edging panel (see chart 4, page 67). Finish by weaving in all ends neatly on wrong side.

Adastra, Chart 1

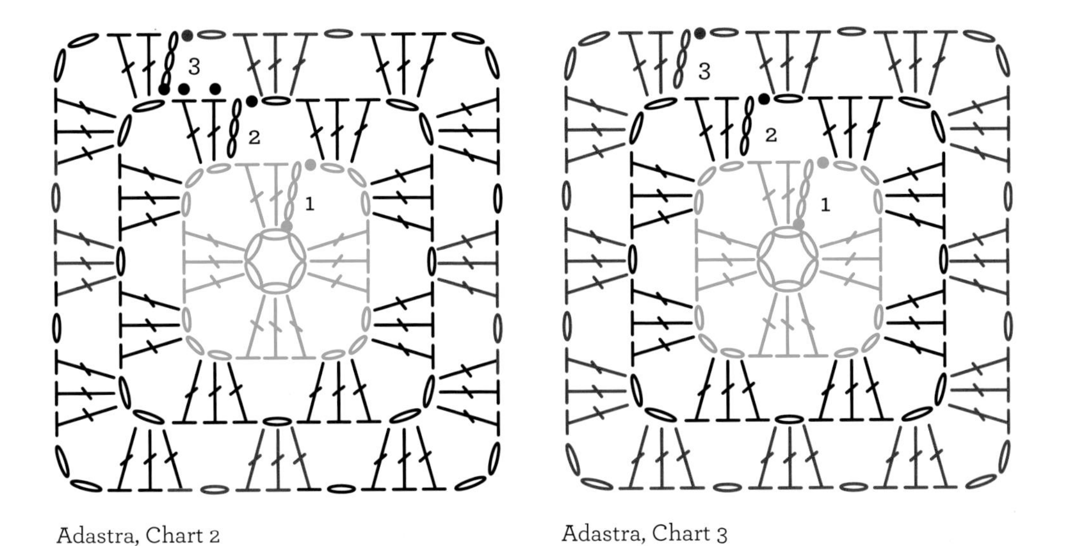


Adastra, Chart 2

Adastra, Chart 3

Substitute the first three rounds on Chart 1 with these variations to create different types of stars.

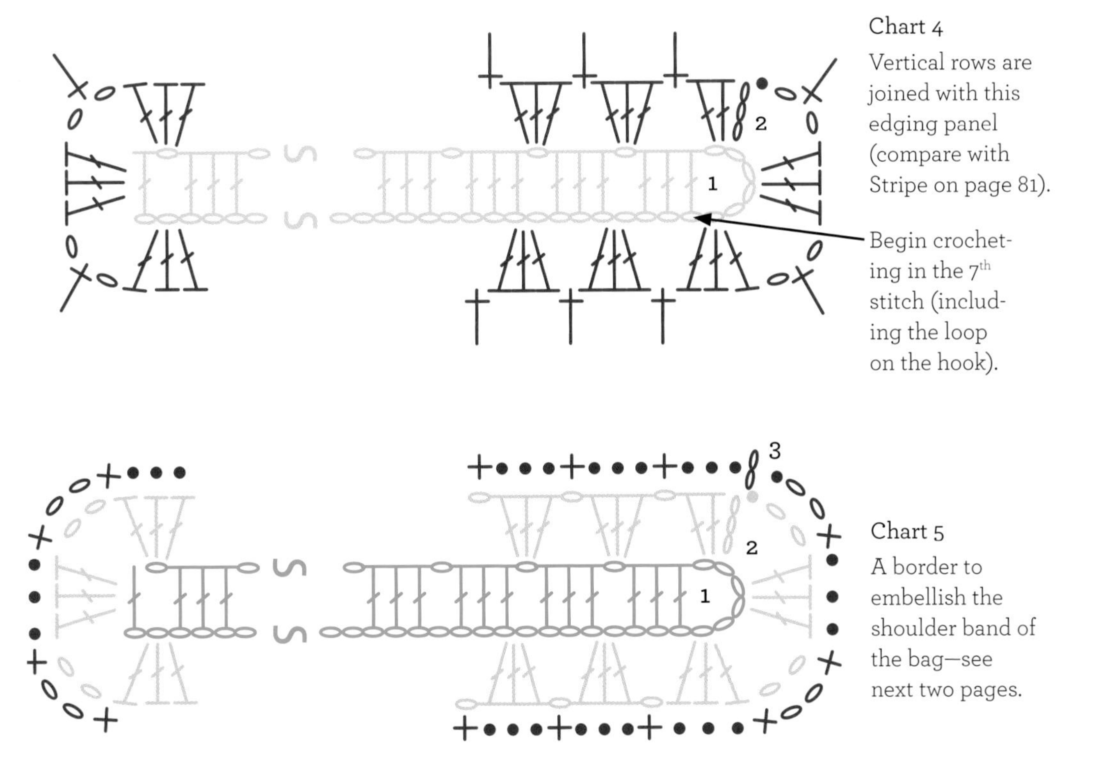


Chart 4

Vertical rows are joined with this edging panel (compare with Stripe on page 81).

Begin crocheting in the 7th stitch (including the loop on the hook).

Chart 5

A border to embellish the shoulder band of the bag—see next two pages.

**Project: Bag**

Crochet four vertical strips with three squares in each. Join the strips, crocheting them together with a red edging panel. Crochet four squares and join them with the red edging. Crochet the two pieces together with a green horizontal edging panel. Crochet the edging panels all around the piece. See schematic below.

For the back and a base, cut pieces of **leather** sized to match the pieces of your bag (my pieces were 9 x 11½ in / 23 x 29 cm and 4¼ x 9 in / 11 x 23 cm). Remember that two of the vertical panels will form the sides of the bag. Punch 1/16 in / 2 mm holes spaced about ¼ in / 5 mm apart (measure from center to center) along the edges. In order to punch the holes in the exact same place on the back and base, first punch the hole in the base. Lay the base as a measure on the edge of the back and mark the place for each hole with a pencil.

Crochet the back and base together with **cotton yarn**, working 2 sc per hole. Continue with 2 sc per hole all around the edges of the leather pieces (in the corners there will be 4 sc per hole). Whip stitch the crochet sections together in the crocheted edges of the leather. Crochet a final round with sc in black all around the top red edging panel of the bag.

Line the bag. I lined the front of my bag with doubled **cotton fabric**, with black towards the crochet and red facing the inside of the bag. Start from the size of the back but add the width of half a crochet square at both sides and at the base. Cut the pieces of cotton fabric (1 black and 2 red pieces) with a 3/8 in / 1 cm seam allowance all around. To add stability, iron on vlieseline interfacing on the wrong side of the black fabric.

Join all three fabrics, the two red fabric pieces with right side facing right side and then the black with the right side out. Machine-stitch along the long sides and one short side using a 3/8 in / 1 cm seam allowance. Press the seams

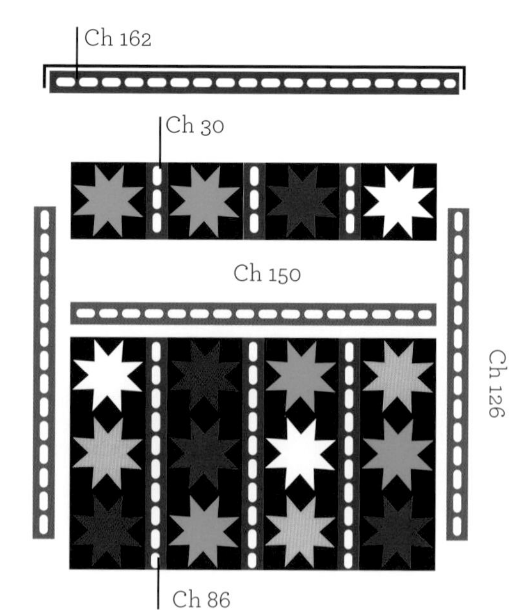

open. Shape the base following the schematic on the opposite side and sew down the corner the same length as the base is wide.

Before you join the bag at the top, make the shoulder band. Crochet a panel following Chart 5 and sew it securely by hand along a **canvas band** (my band was 1½ in / 4 cm wide and 51¼ in / 130 cm long). Sew the shoulder band to the wrong side of the lining, centered at the side seams. Stick about 2 in / 5 cm of the shoulder band down into the bag.

Insert the lining into the bag, folding it down the upper seam allowance, and securely hand-sew the lining to the top edge of the bag. If you want, you can thread a cord through the edging panel and lower chain loops of the bag's side pieces, and then decorate the ends with pompoms.

To make the base sturdier, cut a piece of cardboard the same size as the base and lay it in the bag. For a very snug lining, cover the cardboard with lining fabric.

Shape the base of the lining by sewing it perpendicular to the bottom seam.

My bag was 9 in / 23 cm wide, 15½ in / 39 cm high, and 4¼ in / 11 cm deep.

# Rutger

Easy

**Finished Measurements**
One square measures 4 x 4 in / 10 x 10 cm.

**MATERIALS**

**Yarn:**
CYCA #2 (sport/baby) 6/2 wool yarn (100% wool, 330 yd/302 m / 100 g)

**Yarn Colors:**
My color selection: black, red, and white.

**Crochet Hook:** U. S. size B-1 or C-2 / 2.5 mm: Aero or similar style hook.

I based the idea for Rutger on my own graphic portfolio from my time at Konstfack (the University of Arts, Crafts and Design in Stockholm, Sweden).

Begin each square with a magic ring or ch 6 and close into a ring with 1 sl st.

Now make a square following the chart on the opposite page. Work with red and black at the same time for all rounds on the chart. Carry and catch the unused color as you work. For Rnds 1-5, use the alternate color change method rather than the traditional method (see page 10).

Directly following all the corner chain loops for Rnds 3-5, work 2 dc in the corner chain loop of the previous round, and then skip one dc and work 2 dc in the same stitch. (The reason for working in the same stitch is simply because it's difficult to find the correct loop when the stitches are so close together.)

The squares are joined as you work the last round (see basic instructions on page 12). Cut the black and red strands respectively when you've finished crocheting the edging. Finish by weaving in all ends neatly on WS.

**Edging Panel:** Once all the squares have been joined, work 2 rounds of single crochet all around the piece as a finishing panel. Work the sc through back loops over double crochet; over a chain stitch, insert the hook below it.

**Pattern Effect for Squares:** Use a tapestry needle to run a white strand (27½ in / 70 cm per square) through all the corner chain loops. The sketch below shows the direction of the stitching.

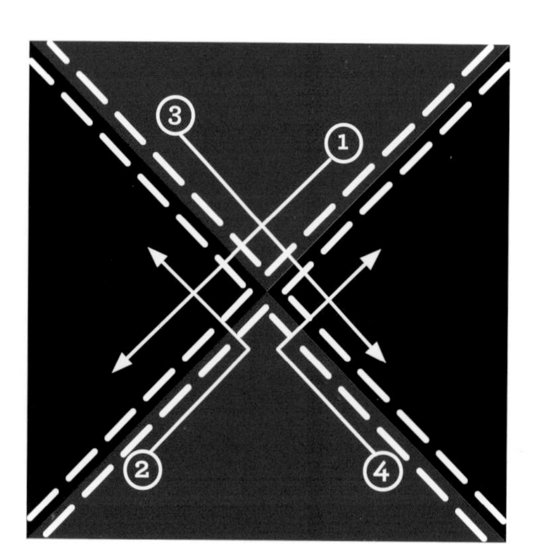


Sew a pattern effect on the squares with white thread. The arrows indicate the order for stitching the lines.

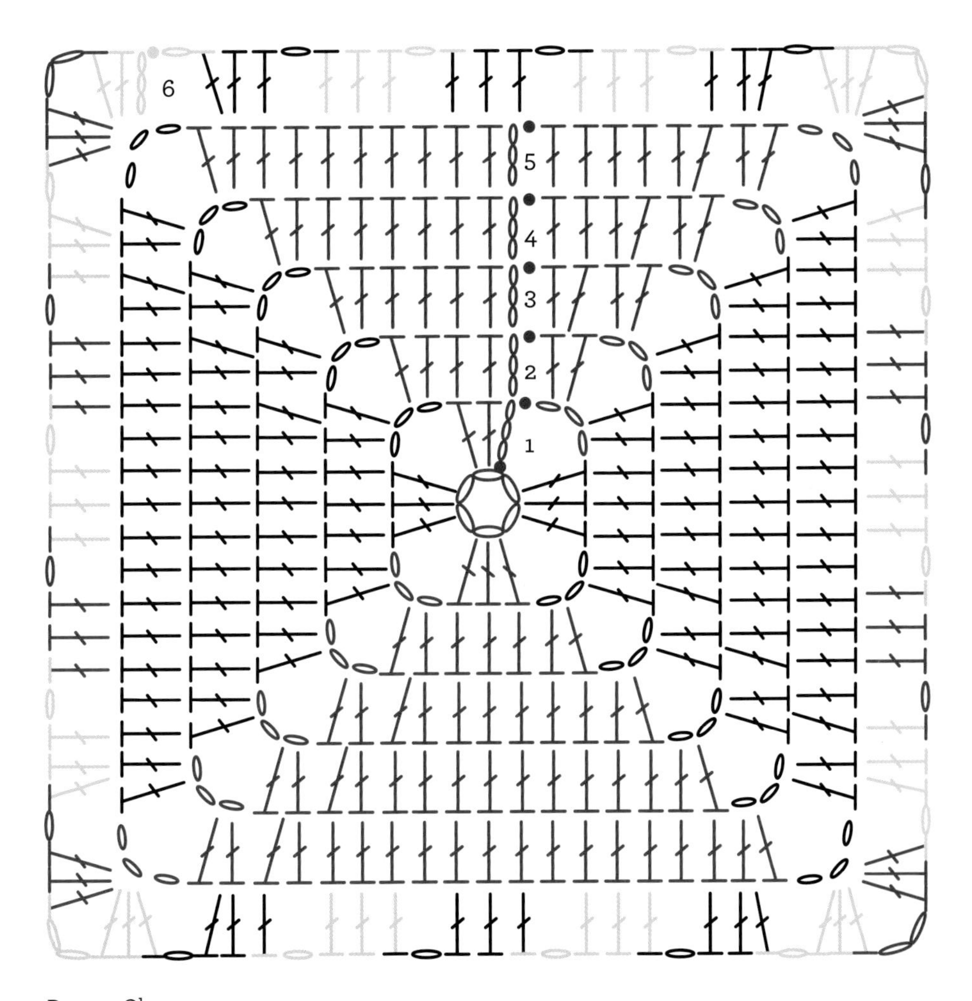


Rutger Chart

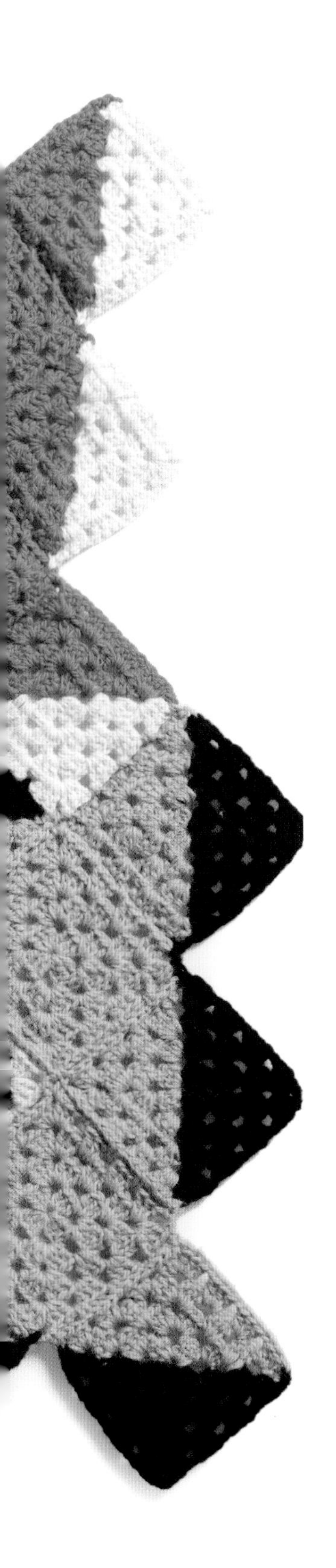

# Pinwheel

Easy

**Finished Measurements**
One square measures 2¾ x 2¾ in / 7 x 7 cm.

MATERIALS
**Yarn:**
CYCA #2 (sport/baby)
6/2 wool yarn (100% wool, 330 yd/302 m / 100 g)

**Yarn Colors:**
My color selection: black, white, and an assortment of colors.
**Crochet Hook:** U. S. size B-1 or C-2 / 2.5 mm: Aero or similar style hook.

I based the idea for Pinwheel on my own graphic portfolio from my time at Konstfack (the University of Arts, Crafts and Design in Stockholm, Sweden).

Begin each square with a magic ring or ch 6 and close into a ring with 1 sl st.

Now make the squares following the charts on the next two pages. Each repeat consists of 13 squares: one following Chart 1, four following Chart 2, and eight with Chart 3. When working the squares from Chart 3, turn the work on every round.

Crochet the squares together as you work Rnd 4, following the basic instructions on page 12. Finish by weaving in all ends neatly on WS.

Pinwheel, Chart 1

Pinwheel, Chart 2

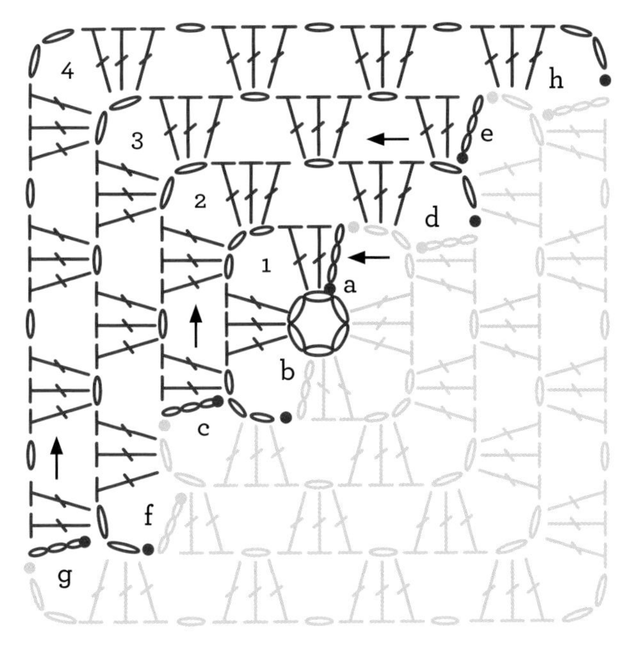

Pinwheel, Chart 3

a) Begin with red (Rnd 1).

b) Begin with white (Rnd 1).

Join the red section with the white section with slip stitches.

c) Turn and continue working with red (Rnd 2).

d) Continue with white (Rnd 2).

Join the red section with the white section with slip stitches.

e) Turn and continue working with red (Rnd 3).

f) Continue with white (Rnd 3).

Join the red section with the white section with slip stitches.

g) Turn and continue working with red (Rnd 4).

h) Continue with white (Rnd 4).

Join the red section with the white section with slip stitches.

# Circular

Easy

**Finished Measurements**
One square measures 3½ x 3½ in / 9 x 9 cm.

**MATERIALS**
**Yarn:**
CYCA #2-3 (sport-DK) 8/4 cotton yarn (100% cotton, 187 yd/170 m / 50 g)

**Yarn Colors:**
My color selection: black, white, and assorted colors.
**Crochet Hook:** U. S. size D-3 / 3 mm: Aero or similar style hook.

My idea derives from graphic design using light and dark contrasts.

Begin each square with a magic ring or ch 6 and close into a ring with 1 sl st.

Now make the squares following the chart on the next page. When you get to Rnd 5, turn the work and continue on the wrong side. Let the black yarn rest while you change to white. You can leave the black yarn on the wrong side (towards you, since you are now working on the wrong side). On Rnd 6, turn the work again and continue on the right side. Cut the white yarn and crochet clockwise. When it's time to pick up the black yarn again, cut the white.

Crochet the squares together as you work Rnd 6, following the basic instructions on page 12. Finish by weaving in all ends neatly on WS.

Circular Chart

# Stripe

Intermediate

**Finished Measurements**
As you like!

**MATERIALS**

**Yarn:**
CYCA #1 (fingering) 18/4 wool yarn (100% wool, 492 yd/450 m / 100 g)

**Yarn Colors:**
My color selection: black, white, red, ochre, and various shades of blue and blue-green.

**Crochet Hook:** U. S. size D-3 / 3 mm: Aero or similar style hook.

**Notions:** A 6 in / 15 cm in diameter piece of leather for base of bag + a leather piece 4¾ in / 12 cm long and 2 in / 5 cm wide for the tassels. A leather cord as a drawstring for the bag. Matching sewing thread. Revolving punch pliers. Glue for leather.

A woven African textile was the inspiration behind this design.

Begin by working a chain with Color 1. The stitch count should be a multiple of 4 sts + 6 turning ch. Crochet strips following Chart 1 on page 83. All the slip stitches on Row 3 are worked through back loops.

Make several strips, choosing as many colors as you want. Follow Chart 2 when joining the strips. Finish by weaving in all ends neatly on WS.

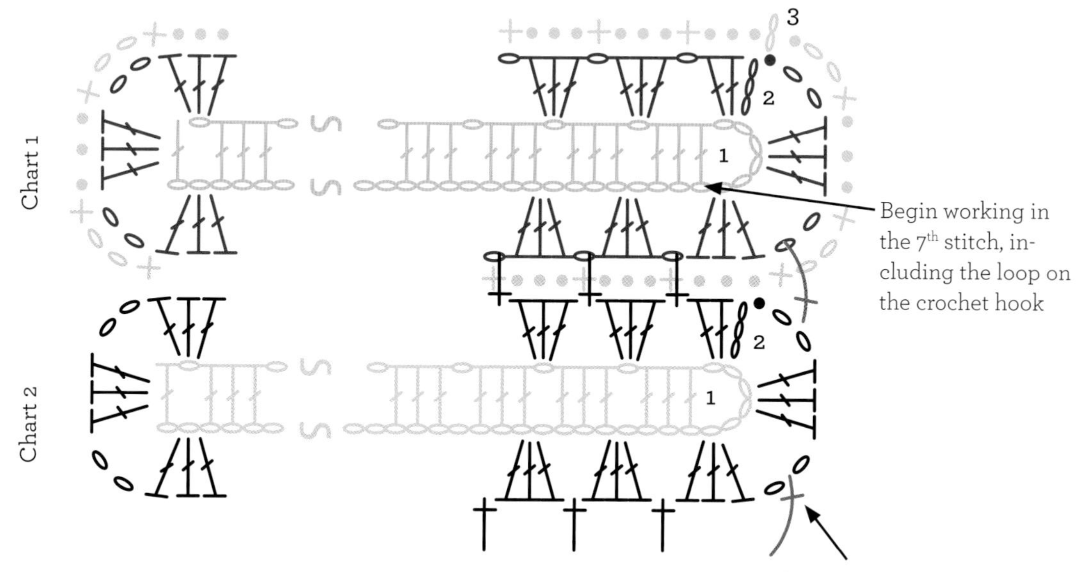

Chart 1
Chart 2
1
2
3
Begin working in the 7th stitch, including the loop on the crochet hook
These dark gray single crochet stitches are worked only when, for example, you are making a bag and need a straight edge to attach the base to.

**Project: Bag**

Ch 82 and work the first strip following Chart 1. Next, make 19 strips in various color combinations = a total of 20 strips. Use Chart 2 for guidance on crocheting the strips together so that, once finished, the piece is a crocheted tube.

**Note:** When joining two strips, work differently at the beginning and end of the row (see the dark gray single crochet stitches to the right of the chart). Later, the side with the extra single crochet stitches will be sewn to the bottom of the bag.

Cut out a base of leather, about 6 in / 15 cm in diameter. Use revolving punch pliers to make holes about 1/16 in / 2 mm wide along the edge, spaced about ¼ in / 5 mm apart (measure from center to center of the holes). I made 90 holes in the base of my bag.

Crochet an edging along the base. On the first round, work 2 sc per hole in the leather base. Finish with 1 sl st into the first stitch of the round. On the second round, decrease the number of stitches by working *7 sc followed by 2 sc together, through back loops.* Repeat * to * around and finish with 1 sl st into the first st of the round. For the third round, decrease the number of stitches by working *6 sc and then 2 sc together, through both loops.* Repeat from * to * around and end with 1 sl st into first st of round.

Turn the tube inside out so the wrong side is facing out. Also turn the leather base inside out so the wrong side of the crocheted edge also faces out. Securely sew the tube to the crocheted edging with whip stitch, as invisibly as possible.

Draw a leather cord through the chain loops a few centimeters from the opening of the bag. Cut a piece of leather 4¾ in / 12 cm long and 2 in / 5 cm wide. Draw a line ¼ in / 0.5 cm from the top edge along the long side. Cut fine fringes up to the marked line. Divide the strip in the middle. Glue the ¼ in / 0.5 cm wide edge and roll the leather fringes around the ends of the leather cord.

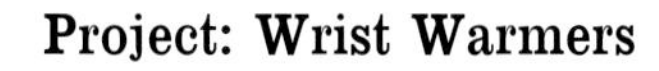

**Project: Wrist Warmers**

Ch 46. Work following the instructions on page 81 and the chart on page 83. **Note:** When joining two strips, you will work the same way at the beginning and end of the row (the dark gray single crochet stitches to the right of the chart are not worked for this project). Sew tiny pompoms on each point of the cuff.

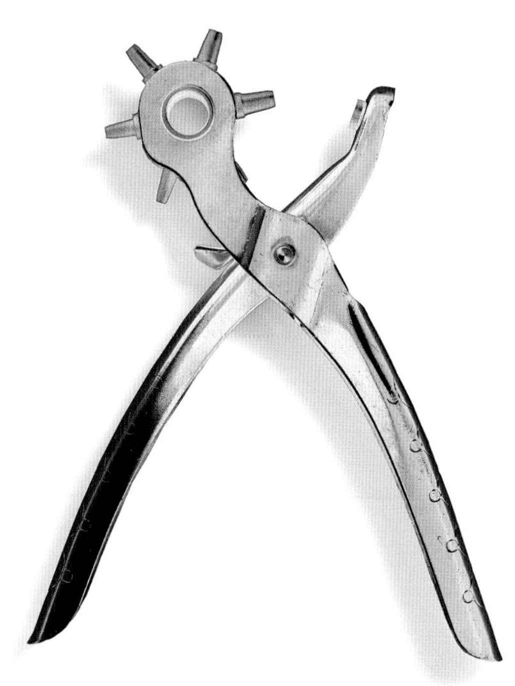

You can punch holes in the leather base with revolving punch pliers.

# Armida

Intermediate

**Finished Measurements**
One square measures 7½ x 7½ in / 19 x 19 cm.
The edging is 3¼ in / 8 cm wide.

**MATERIALS**

**Yarn:**
CYCA #2 (sport/baby)
6/2 wool yarn (100% wool, 330 yd/302 m / 100 g)

**Yarn Colors:**
My color selection: black, white, and an assortment of colors.

**Crochet Hook:** U. S. size B-1 or C-2 / 2.5 mm: Aero or similar style hook.

I took my inspiration from glazed tiles and mosaic designs.

Begin each square with a magic ring or ch 6 and close into a ring with 1 sl st. Work each square following Chart 1 on the next page. On all the even-numbered rounds, leave the unused color aside (do not carry it around).

When you've crocheted as many squares as you want, it's time to assemble them. Block the squares before you join them so the work will be easier and neater. If, for example, you have a Styrofoam disk or something similar, you can push double-pointed needles into the corners of a marked outline of the correct size and then stack the squares on the needles. Spray the squares with a little water and then leave them until dry. When blocking is finished, use white yarn to sew the squares together from the right side with five whip stitches in each chain loop.

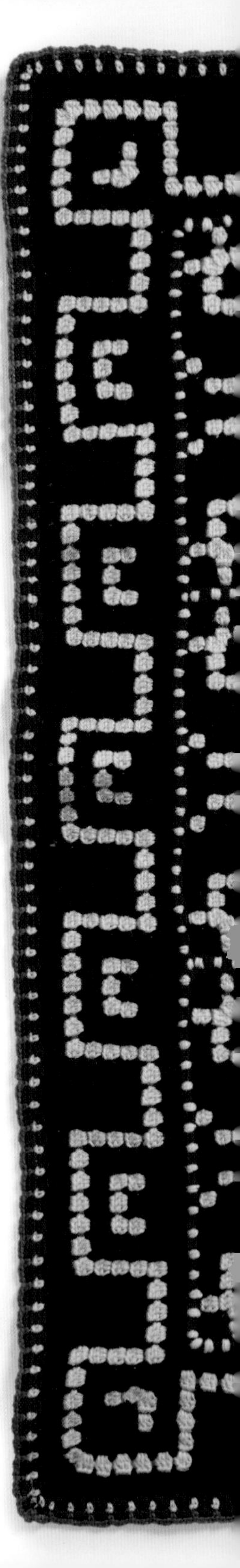

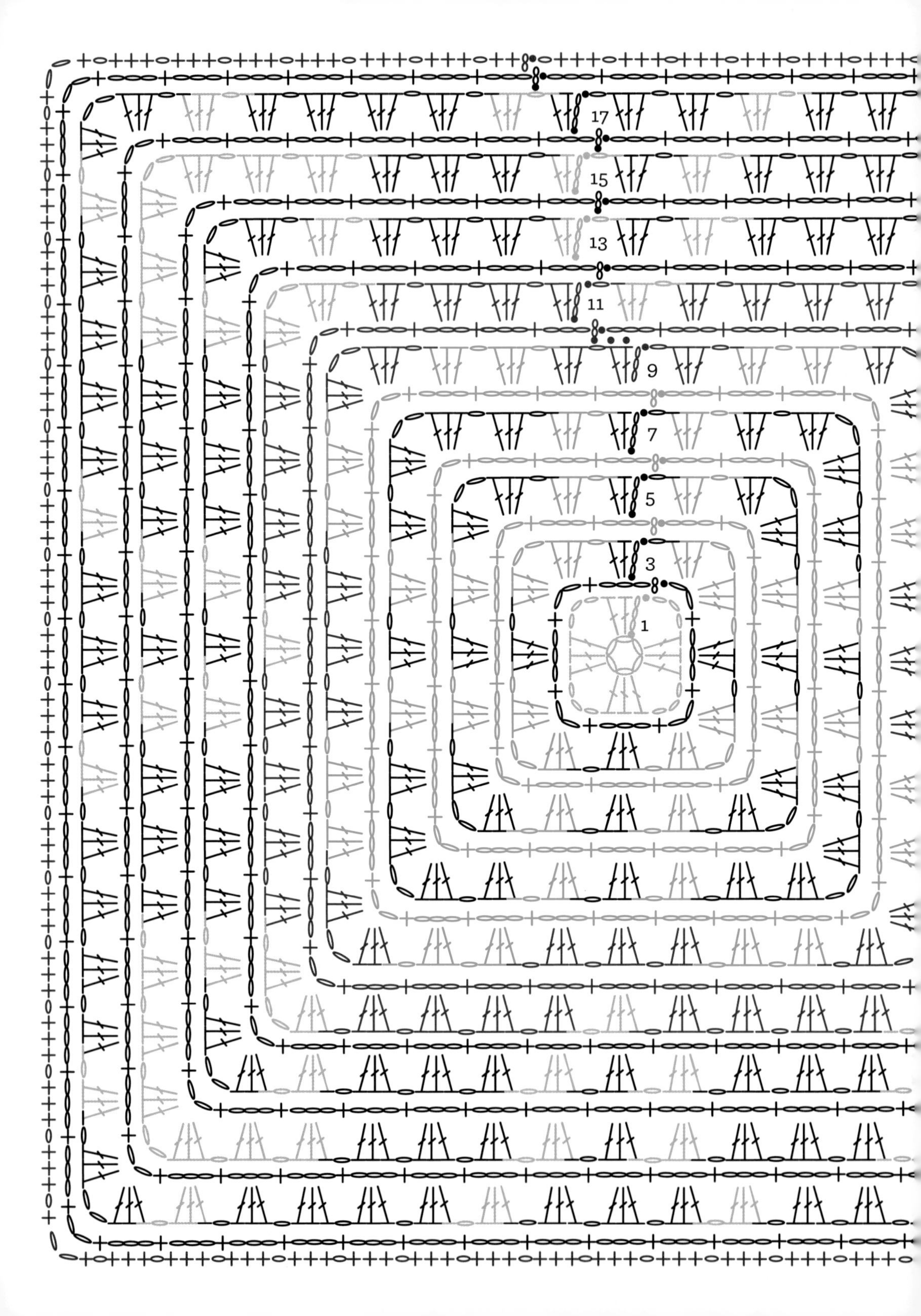
17
15
13
11
9
7
5
3
1

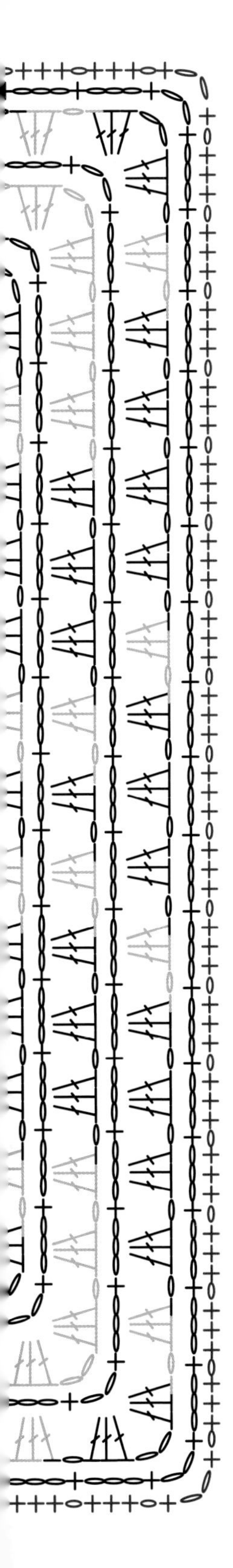

Armida, Chart 1

When all the squares have been joined, finish with an edging panel all around, following Chart 2 on pages 92-93. When working the rounds with tips, leave the unused yarn to "rest" at beginning of round.

To have an even frame around the squares at the edge, finish by sewing five whip stitches with white yarn over the single crochet stitches joining the edging panel to the squares.

**Project: Mat**

This mosaic style pattern makes Armida especially charming as a mat. The size of the mat depends on how many squares you crochet. For a bathmat, for example, crochet six squares, using cotton yarn instead of wool.

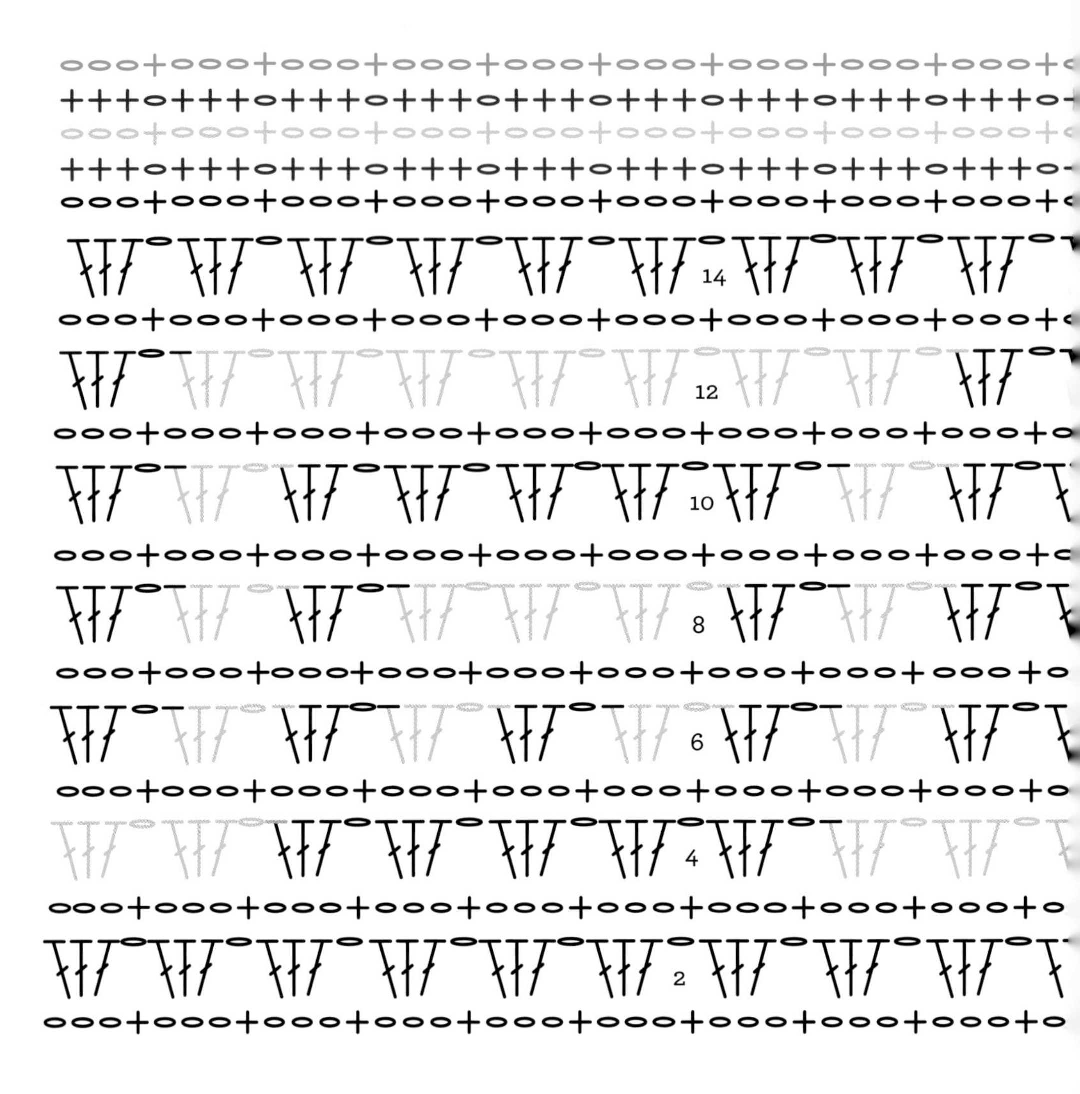


Armida, Chart 2

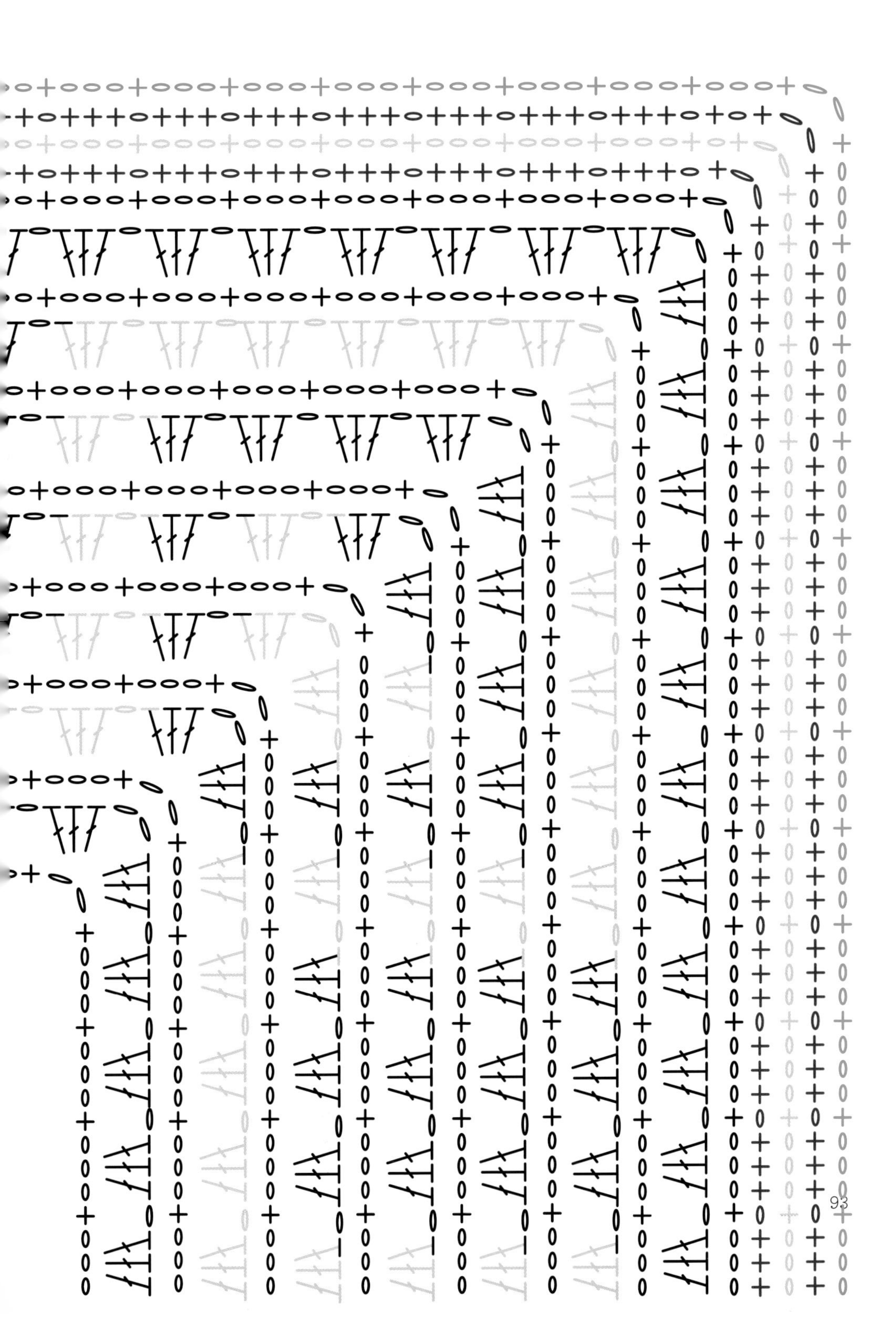

| # Beata | Intermediate to Experienced |
|---|---|

**Finished Measurements**
One square measures 4¾ x 4¾ in / 12 x 12 cm.

**MATERIALS**

**Yarn:**
CYCA #2 (sport/baby) 6/2 wool yarn (100% wool, 330 yd/302 m / 100 g)

**Yarn Colors:**
My color selection: red, white, and gray.

**Crochet Hook:** U. S. size B-1 or C-2 / 2.5 mm: Aero or similar style hook.

This square is a variation on Special (see page 46). The design differs from Special in that it's worked as a classic granny square on all rounds.

Begin each square with a magic ring or ch 6 and close into a ring with 1 sl st. Work each square following the chart on page 96.

Crochet the squares together as you work Rnd 9 following the basic instructions on page 12. Finish by weaving in all ends neatly on WS.

Beata Chart

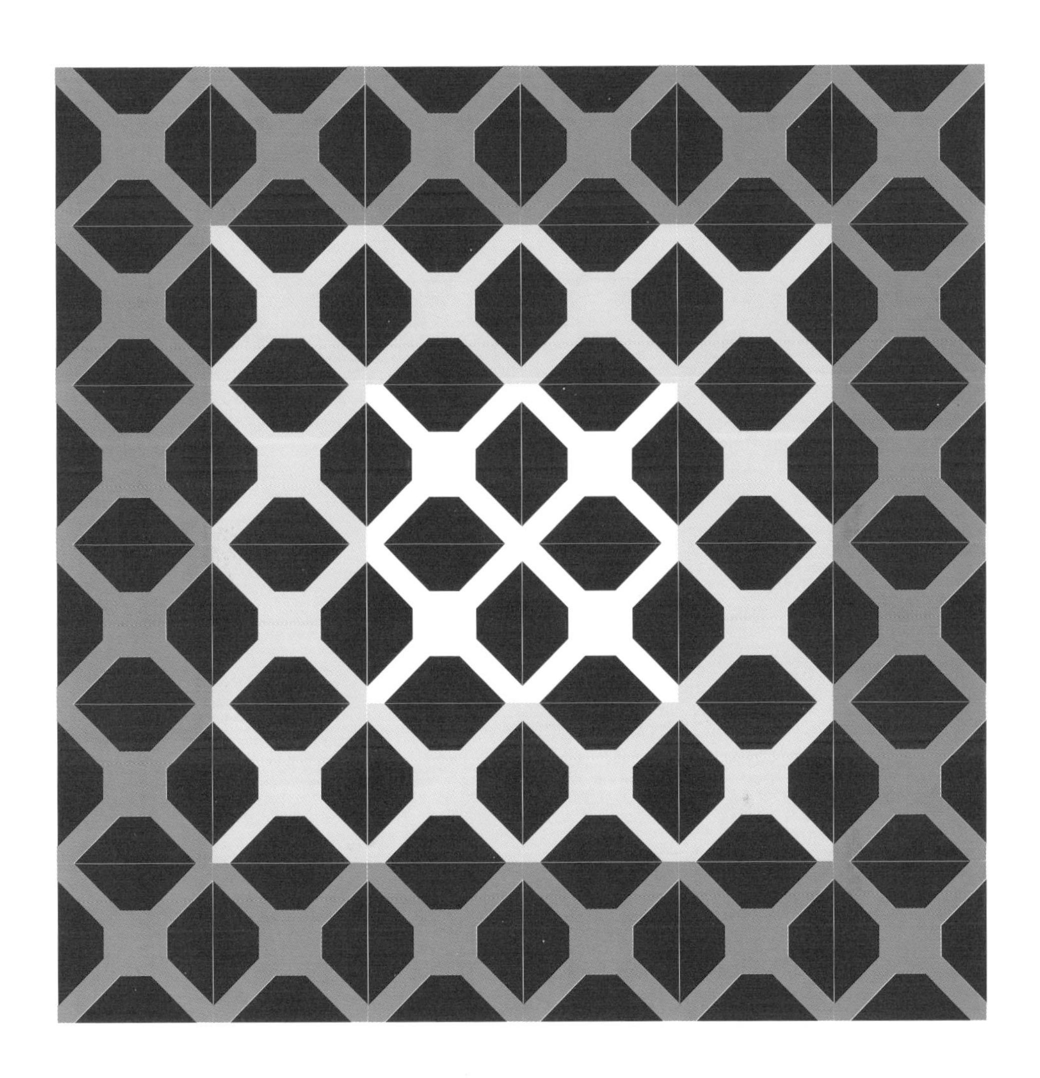

Color effects on the larger surfaces of Beata

When I designed this pattern, I wanted the squares to be increasingly dark towards the outer edges. If you don't want that effect, you can work with only two colors throughout.

# Goose-Eye

Easy

**Finished Measurements**
One square measures 2¾ x 2¾ in / 7 x 7 cm.

**MATERIALS**
**Yarn:**
CYCA #2 (sport/baby) 6/2 wool yarn (100% wool, 330 yd/302 m / 100 g)

**Yarn Colors:**
My color selection: black and white.
**Crochet Hook:** U. S. size B-1 or C-2 / 2.5 mm: Aero or similar style hook.

The idea for this square's look was adapted from a woven twill fabric. I twisted and turned the motif so it formed rhomboid shapes with an optical illusion effect.

Begin each square with a magic ring or ch 6 and close into a ring with 1 sl st. Crochet the squares following the charts on pages 100-101. Each square has 5 rounds and is worked with 2 colors per round throughout.

Crochet the squares together as you work Rnd 5 following the basic instructions on page 12. Finish by weaving in all ends neatly on WS.

Goose-Eye, Chart 1

### Black and white squares

This pattern consists of two repeats. The first repeat has four squares made following Chart 1. The second repeat also has four squares, but they are worked following Chart 2. Turn and mirror-image the squares in the repeats to create the pattern.

Goose-Eye, Chart 2

Red and white squares

This pattern consists of two repeats. The first repeat has four squares, two following Chart 1 and two following Chart 2. The second repeat has four squares, all worked following Chart 2. Turn and mirror-image the squares in the repeats to create the pattern.

# Baltazar

Difficult Even for Experienced Crocheters

**Finished Measurements**
One repeat measures 5¾ x 3¾ in / 14.5 x 9.5 cm.

**MATERIALS**
**Yarn:**
CYCA #1 (fingering) 18/4 wool yarn (100% wool, 492 yd/450 m / 100 g)
**Yarn Colors:**
My color selection: red, white, and black.
**Crochet Hook:** U. S. size D-3 / 3 mm: Aero or similar style hook.
**Notions:** Pillow form slightly larger than pillow cover. A piece of red *vadmal* (woven and then felted fabric) or felt 1¼ in / 3 cm larger on each side than cover size. Cotton lining fabric ³/₈ in / 1 cm larger on each side than cover size. Matching sewing thread. Black leather (you will need enough to cut four strips 1¼ in / 3 cm wide and 2¾ in / 7 cm long) and silver-dyed leather (you will need enough to cut four strips, ⁵/₈ in / 1.5 cm wide and 2 in / 5 cm long).
Wire-cutting scissors.
Glue for leather.

A Baltic pattern lies behind this design concept.

Begin each square with a magic ring or ch 6 and close into a ring with 1 sl st. Crochet each square following Chart 1 on the page opposite. The squares are crocheted together through the corner chain loops.

### Project: Pillow Cover

If you want to make a pillow cover (see photo on pages 108-109), crochet nine squares following Chart 1, four squares with Chart 2, and six squares with Chart 3. Crochet the squares together in the corner chain loops following the illustrations on page 106. Next, crochet eight half-squares following Chart 4, six small half-squares following Chart 5, and four corner squares following Chart 6. The half-squares will be

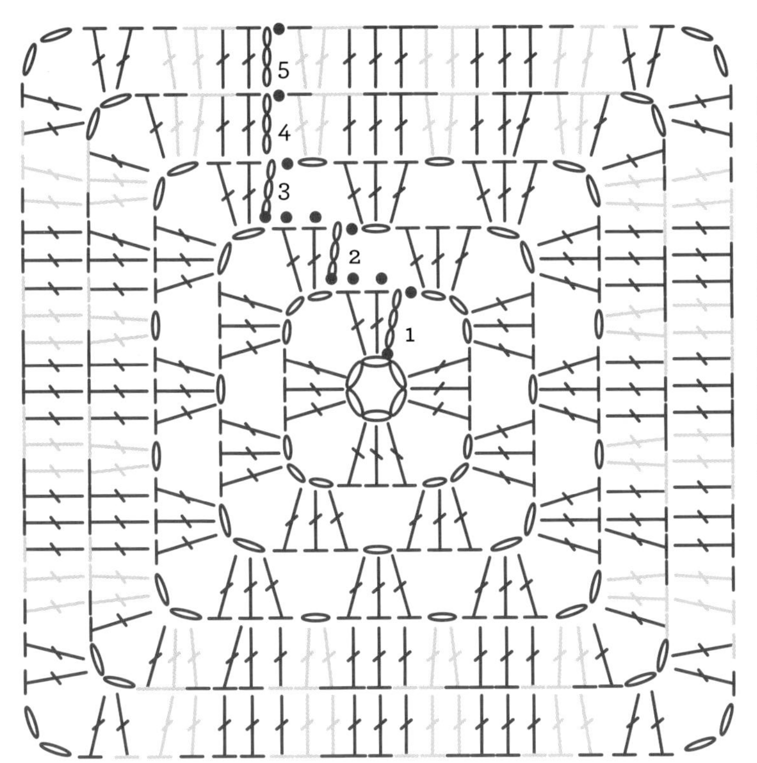


Baltazar, Chart 1

Immediately after the corner chain loops during Rnd 4, work 3 dc in the previous round's corner chain loop, skip a dc, and then work 2 dc in the same stitch. (The reason for working in the same stitch is simply because it's difficult to find the correct loop when the stitches are so close together.)

Baltazar, Chart 2

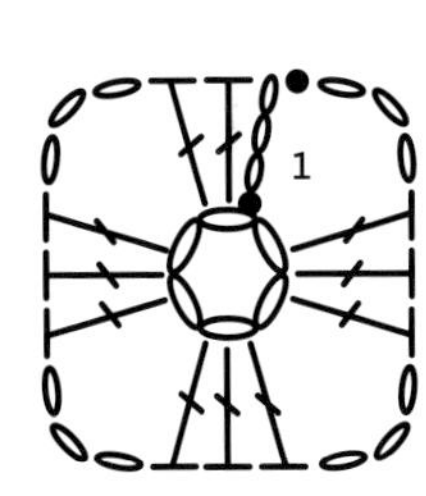


Baltazar, Chart 3

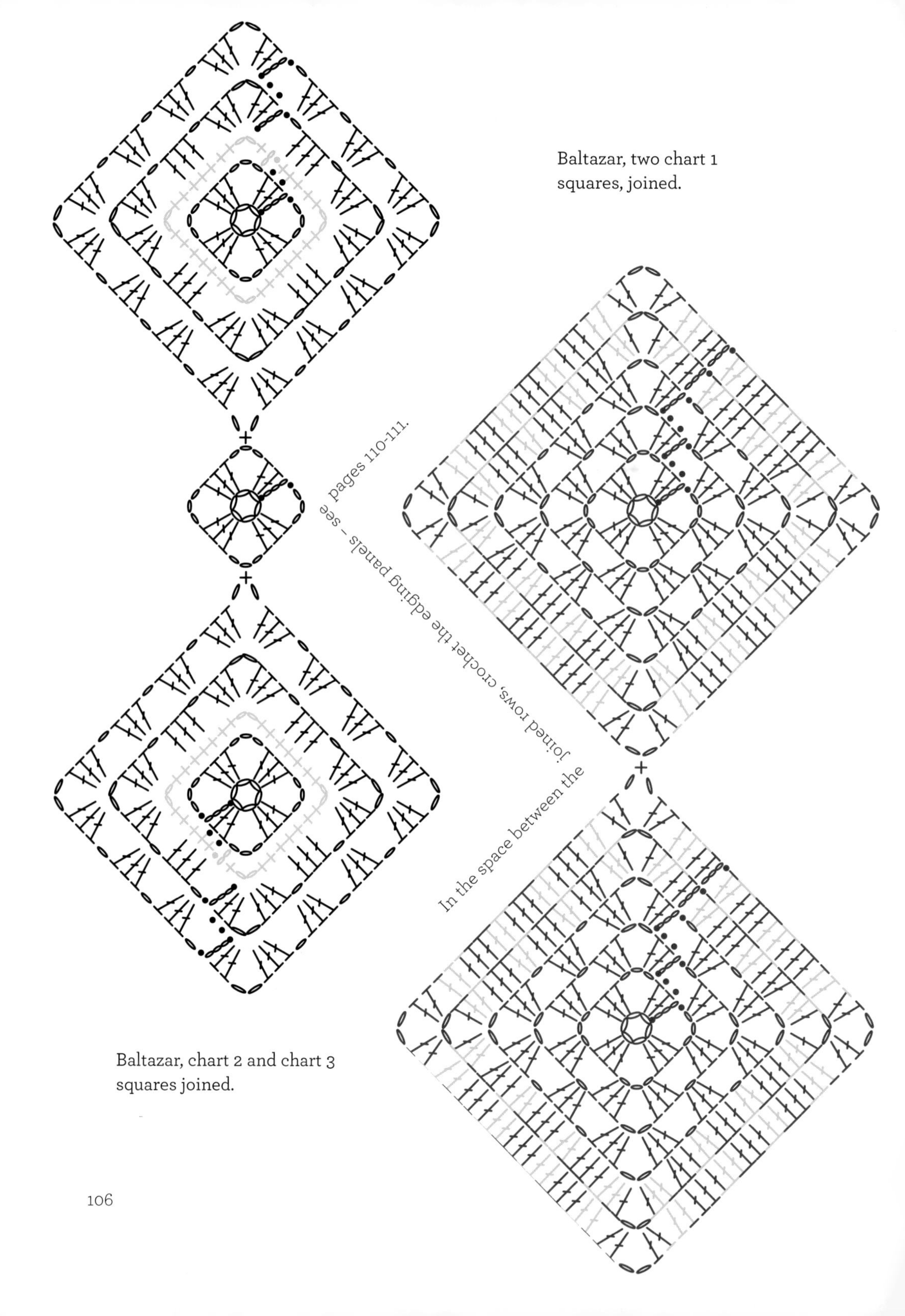

Baltazar, two chart 1 squares, joined.

In the space between the joined rows, crochet the edging panels – see pages 110-111.

Baltazar, chart 2 and chart 3 squares joined.

### Chart 4—Edge Squares

The three single crochet stitches and the three double crochet stitches that begin and end Rows 2, 3, and 4 are all worked in the first stitch of the previous row.

Turn the work on Row 3 and crochet on the wrong side. Row 4 is worked on the right side.

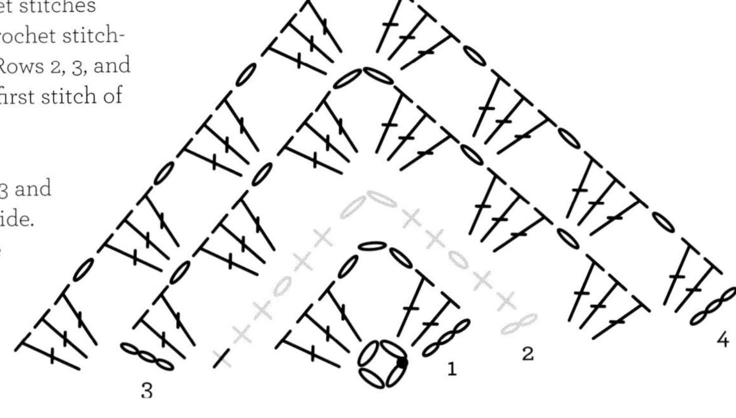


### Chart 5—Edge Square

### Chart 6—Corner

The three single crochet stitches and the three double crochet stitches that begin and end Rows 2, 3, and 4 are all worked in the first stitch of the previous row.

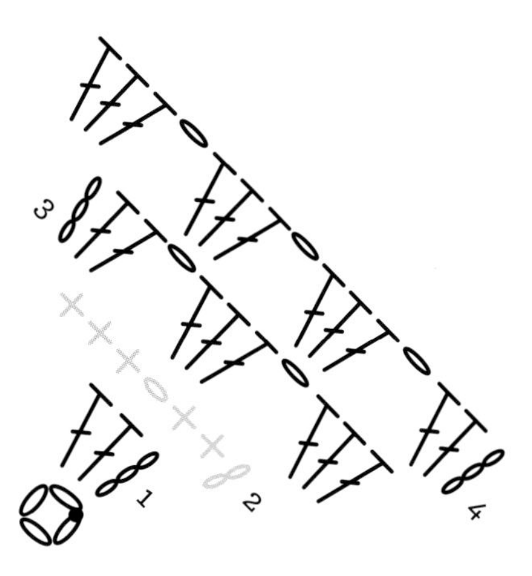

placed along the edges of the pillow cover. Crochet Edging Panel 1 around the black squares. Crochet Edging Panel 2 around the red squares, and on the last round join Panel 2 to Panel 1. When you've finished crocheting the entire piece, you can even out the outer edges with a round of single crochet all around and then another round of half-double crochet.

**Finishing the Pillow Cover**

Measure the crocheted front and cut a backing of red *vadmal* (woven and then felted fabric) or felt 1¼ in / 3 cm larger in each direction. Cut **cotton lining fabric** with an extra 3/8 in / 1 cm all around.

Lay the lining centered on the felted piece. Fold the long sides of the felted piece to overlap the lining by ¾ in / 2 cm and pin. Fold one short side over the same way and pin it. Using small running stitches positioned 3/8 in / 1 cm in from the turned edge, sew the felted piece and lining fabric together on three sides of the cover. Sew the corners together as invisibly and finely as possible. If the corner is too thick, carefully cut away a little of the felted piece on the underlying layer.

Place the crocheted front on the lining and pin. The front should lie about 3/8 in / 1 cm inside the outer edge of the felted piece.

Edging Panels 1 and 2

These edging panels are crocheted on the right side of the piece. Work all stitches through back loops. Begin in the top corner chain loop. On Rnd 1, work the slip stitches rather loosely or with a hook one size larger than for the rest of the piece. Crochet all the rows at the same time in stages. That way, you'll minimize the risk of losing your place, and if you've made a mistake, you'll realize it relatively quickly.

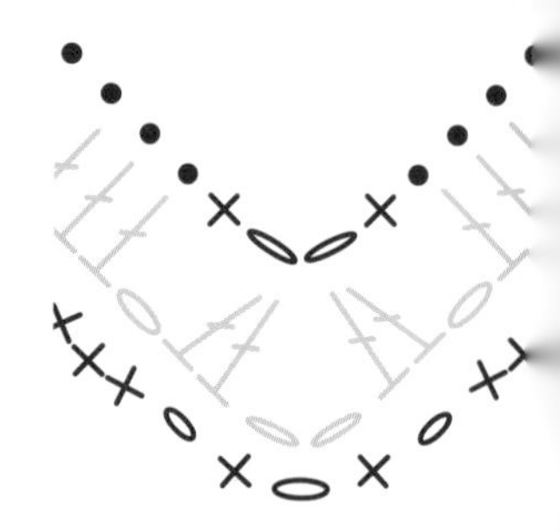

Edging Panel 1

The panel is crocheted outside the row of black squares.

Edging Panel 2

The panel is crocheted outside the row of red squares.
As you work Row 4, crochet the panel together withEdging Panel 1. The letters mark how the joining happens at the trickier spots.

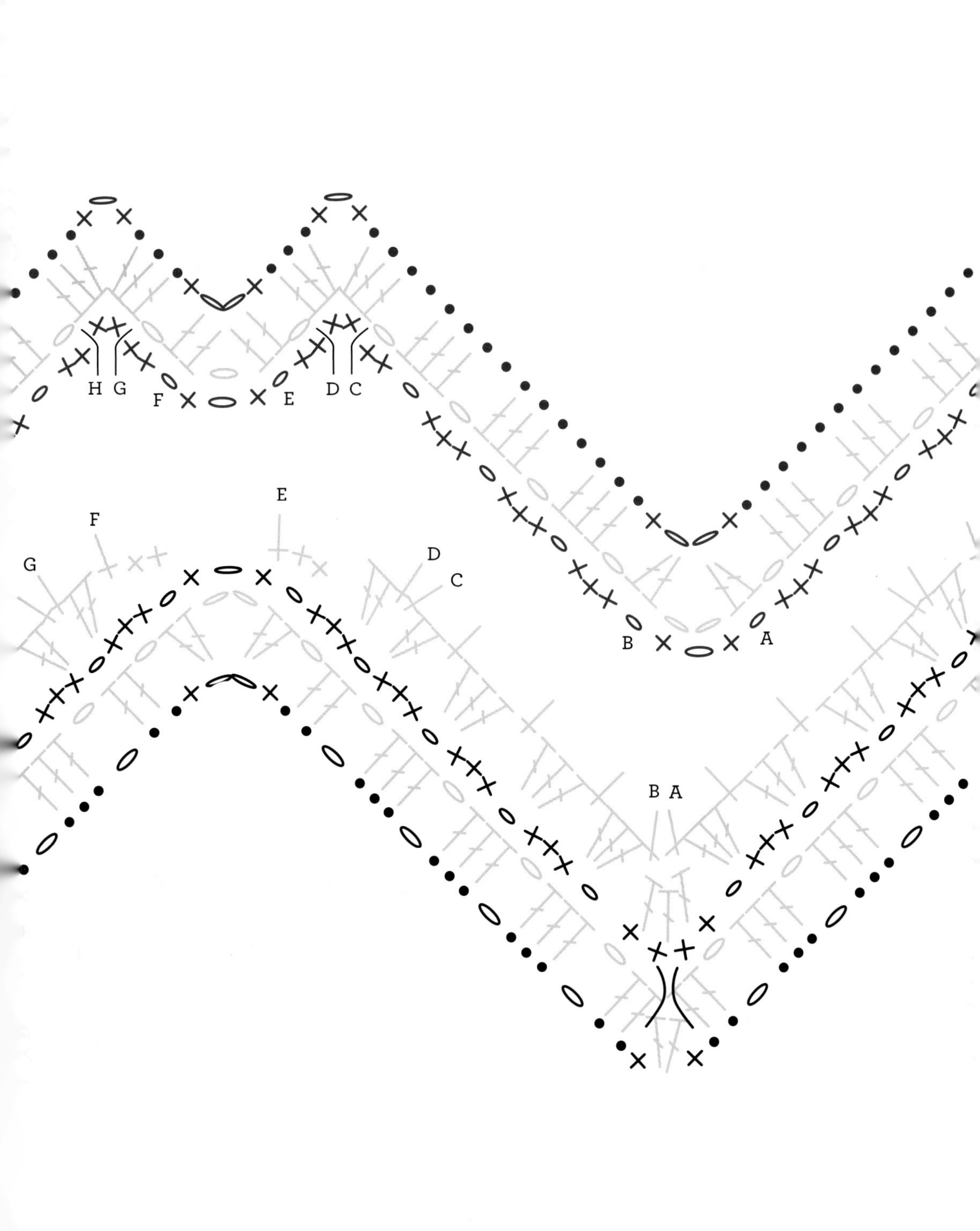

H G
F
E
D C
G
F
E
D
C
B
A
B A

The Baltazar pillow cover is composed of whole, half, and quarter squares joined altogether with two different edging panels.

**Leather Tassels:** With wire cutting scissors, cut four black strips of leather (1¼ in / 3 cm wide and 2¾ in / 7 cm long) and cut four silver leather strips (5/8 in / 1.5 cm wide and 2 in / 5 cm long). With red yarn, crochet four cords with about 30 chain stitches with red yarn. Sew the cords using sewing thread in the center of the silver strips. Glue the silver strips onto the black leather strips. Securely sew the leather tassels onto the two sewn corners so that they hide the folded corner.

Sew the crocheted front. In order to get a piping effect, sew in the previous seam, 3/8 in / 1 cm in from the folded felted edges. Begin sewing 1¼ in / 4 cm from the short side (which hasn't been folded in yet). Sew with small whip stitches and use sewing thread the same color as the felted piece. The crocheted front's corners should lie over the leather tassels.

When you are sewing all around, stop when 1¼ in / 4 cm remain from the edge of the short side. Insert the pillow form, which should be slightly larger than the cover so it will fill out the corners well. Fold the short side in and sew the edge together as previously and sew on the rest of the crochet front. Finish by attaching the last two leather tassels.